CAMBRIDGE LIBRARY COLLECTION

Books of enduring scholarly value

Archaeology

The discovery of material remains from the recent or the ancient past has always been a source of fascination, but the development of archaeology as an academic discipline which interpreted such finds is relatively recent. It was the work of Winckelmann at Pompeii in the 1760s which first revealed the potential of systematic excavation to scholars and the wider public. Pioneering figures of the nineteenth century such as Schliemann, Layard and Petrie transformed archaeology from a search for ancient artifacts, by means as crude as using gunpowder to break into a tomb, to a science which drew from a wide range of disciplines - ancient languages and literature, geology, chemistry, social history - to increase our understanding of human life and society in the remote past.

A Guide to the
Prehistoric Rock Engravings in the Italian Maritime Alps

In the mountainous border region between France and Italy lies the Vallée des Merveilles. Still surprisingly remote, and dominated by Mont Bégo, it contains alpine meadows, rare flora and fauna, spectacular glaciated rock formations, and over 35,000 Bronze Age rock engravings that are only free of snow for a few months of the year. Though this major archaeological site was mentioned in print around 1650, the first thorough guidebook was published in 1913 by Clarence Bicknell (1842–1918), a Cambridge graduate and Anglican clergyman who had settled on the Riviera around 1880. Bicknell published several books on the botany of the region, but it was not until the 1890s that he began in earnest to explore the petroglyphs, a project he continued into his seventies. He built up a collection of over 12,000 drawings, rubbings and photographs, which form the basis of the 46 plates that illustrate this book.

Cambridge University Press has long been a pioneer in the reissuing of out-of-print titles from its own backlist, producing digital reprints of books that are still sought after by scholars and students but could not be reprinted economically using traditional technology. The Cambridge Library Collection extends this activity to a wider range of books which are still of importance to researchers and professionals, either for the source material they contain, or as landmarks in the history of their academic discipline.

Drawing from the world-renowned collections in the Cambridge University Library and other partner libraries, and guided by the advice of experts in each subject area, Cambridge University Press is using state-of-the-art scanning machines in its own Printing House to capture the content of each book selected for inclusion. The files are processed to give a consistently clear, crisp image, and the books finished to the high quality standard for which the Press is recognised around the world. The latest print-on-demand technology ensures that the books will remain available indefinitely, and that orders for single or multiple copies can quickly be supplied.

The Cambridge Library Collection brings back to life books of enduring scholarly value (including out-of-copyright works originally issued by other publishers) across a wide range of disciplines in the humanities and social sciences and in science and technology.

A Guide to the
Prehistoric Rock Engravings
in the Italian Maritime Alps

Clarence Bicknell

CAMBRIDGE
UNIVERSITY PRESS

CAMBRIDGE
UNIVERSITY PRESS

University Printing House, Cambridge, CB2 8BS, United Kingdom

Cambridge University Press is part of the University of Cambridge.
It furthers the University's mission by disseminating knowledge in the pursuit of
education, learning and research at the highest international levels of excellence.

www.cambridge.org
Information on this title: www.cambridge.org/9781108082587

© in this compilation Cambridge University Press 2015

This edition first published 1913
This digitally printed version 2015

ISBN 978-1-108-08258-7 Paperback

C. BICKNELL

A GUIDE

to

THE PREHISTORIC

ROCK ENGRAVINGS

in

The Italian Maritime Alps

BORDIGHERA
Printed by GIUSEPPE BESSONE
1913

CONTENTS

Explanation of the Plates

PREFACE

So much has lately been written about the Prehistoric Rock-Engravings in the Italian Maritime Alps, that an apology seems to be needed for publishing anything more; but as I am now, after twelve years of almost continuous explorations, pretty well acquainted with the whole region, and think that there is not much more to be discovered, I wish to say my last word upon the subject, and gather together the substance of what I have already printed in many pamphlets, taking advantage of what has been written by others, and especially by those scientific visitors who under our guidance have seen some small portion of the vast region where the engravings are to be found. It is not at all likely that anyone will ever be able to devote so many years as we have done to the neighbourhood, and we therefore hope that this book will serve as a guide to those who may come in the future, and enable them to find without great loss of time what is most worth seeing. Though I am alone chiefly responsible for the following pages, I use the word 'we' in speaking of our explorations and discoveries, because I have nearly always been accompanied by my Italian friend Signor Luigi Pollini, for very many years my faithful assistant at home, and my helpful companion when travelling and botanizing in Europe, Africa and Asia. Without his quicker eyes, nimbler feet, and indefatigable assistance, very many of the rocks most difficult of access, and of the figures cut upon them, would not have been discovered. He has climbed steep and slippery places where I was loth to go, and taken copies and made photographs of the figures there, and has never been weary when I could walk or work no more. I therefore take this opportunity of thanking him for the great service he has rendered me, without which a large part of what follows could not have been written. I also desire to thank my friend Professor Arturo Issel for the encouragement he has always given me to continue the explorations, and to publish from time to time some account of them.

As the figures on the rocks vary greatly in size, from a few centimetres to a few metres, and we have been obliged to place the copies of those which we have chosen for our plates in close juxtaposition, we have drawn them by eye, not always as well as we could have wished, but we believe accurately. The labour of reducing so many by means of a pantograph would have been very great, and we should have been obliged to use a great number of different scales. We have therefore given, for those of our readers who care to know the actual dimensions of the original rubbings, their vertical and horizontal lengths in centimetres. By this method we think it is easier to grasp at once what is the real size of the originals, than if one is told that the figures of the plates are 1/8, 1/10, or whatever it may be.

We have to thank Signor Benigni of Bordighera for the large photographs; the small ones were taken by ourselves.

Since the following pages were written we have spent another summer in Val Casterino. In Val Fontanalba we have copied about a hundred more figures, chiefly small or indistinct ones, but in the Meraviglie region we have discovered some engraved rocks on the slopes of M. Bego high above Laghi Lunghi and others above the right bank of the Vallone, sone of them very interesting ones, and have added some 250 figures to our collection, so that our total amounts to nearly 5150 for the Meraviglie, over 7000 for Val Fontanalba, about 130 for Val Valauretta and 20 for Col Sabbione, in all more than 12,000.

CLARENCE BICKNELL.

Bordighera, 1913.

CHAPTER I.

The Regions of the Prehistoric Rock Engravings
in the Italian Maritime Alps.

Although there is no difficulty in reaching the prehistoric rock-engravings in the Italian Maritime Alps, and the mountain paths which lead to them are clearly marked on the maps, they have not been so often visited as might have been expected, seeing that their existence has been well known for over forty years. A good many alpine climbers have passed by a few of them on their way to the higher peaks, or gone somewhat out of their route to pay them a hurried visit, and a few men of science, particularly interested in prehistoric studies, have made excursions for the purpose; but it is not even yet generally known what large numbers of these engravings exist, nor does it seem to be fully realized over what vast tracts of valley and mountain sides they are thickly spread. Perhaps too much has been said about the " indescribable horror," as one author wrote, of the region, and too little about the great variety and beauty of the scenery, with peaks and precipices, streams and lakes. The weather has been mentioned as exceptionally stormy there, whereas in fact the summer climate on the southern side of the central chain is usually all that can be desired. It is never hot, and two consecutive days of rain are very rare. Afternoon thunderstorms or heavy showers are not uncommon in June and part of July, but these are of short duration, and the remainder of the summer and the months of September and even of October are generally perfect for mountain excursions. Probably the chief reason for the paucity of visitors is that these regions are at some distance from habitations, and we may add that so much is being done and is to be done both in France and Italy, that workers in the prehistoric field have no time to visit a region already more or less described.

Until lately there has been no convenient starting place for the rock-figures nearer than San Dalmazzo in the Roja valley. This is a pretty spot among the chestnut trees, 696 metres above the sea, with very good hotel, villas, custom-house, post-office and restaurants. It is much frequented in the summer months, chiefly by visitors from the coast. It is distant 43 kilometres from Ventimiglia, whence several auto-omnibuses run daily in about two hours, and about 5 kilometres south of the picturesque and interesting town of Tenda. Autocars also run from Nice in about six hours. Travellers from Piedmont will take the train to Cuneo, and from there by rail pass through the long tunnel under the Col di Tenda to reach Vievola, the present terminus, but the line will soon be opened to Tenda. At Vievola station carriages or omnibus may be found for San Dalmazzo, 9 kilometres down the valley. From there the nearest rock-engravings are distant about 5 hours by mule or on foot, and the farthest 6 or 7, so that not much can be seen by anyone staying at San Dalmazzo if the return there must be made the same day. A night's lodging of some kind has often but not always been obtainable at the mines of Tenda or at S. Maria Maddalena in the Casterino valley, both of them 3 hours distant from S. Dalmazzo, but lately restaurants have been opened at these two places, where very fair accomodation may be found, and the inscribed rocks have become much more accessible.

They are nearly all situated at the foot of Monte Bego or near it, north, south, east and west. This mountain, 2873 metres high, has been called the Righi of the Maritime Alps, being a very attractive summit to ordinarily good walkers, and presenting no sort of difficulty. From its top there is a magnificent view of the Maritime Alps and of the seaboard from the Maure mountains in France to the Apuan Alps; Corsica is visible across the sea to the south, and to the north the plains of Piedmont with Monte Viso and the distant Monte Rosa. Monte Bego and its higher neighbour Gran Capelet 2927 m. are visible from the railway between Nice and Antibes, and from most of the higher hills near Ventimiglia and Bordighera. They are particularly striking from the bridge crossing the Roja at Ventimiglia, as they are covered with snow all through the winter and far into the summer. The one on the right is Monte Bego, with rounded shoulder; that to the left with pointed triangular summit is Gran Capelet. The passage of the Col di Tenda at the head of the Roja valley was known in very early times, and though we have no evidence that Ventimiglia was the starting place for those who crossed from the sea coast into the plains of Piedmont, we may well believe that if they did so, the sight of these two high peaks facing them and seeming to block their way, would have greatly impressed them. The peep of Ventimiglia, with its houses glistening in the sunlight, is very beautiful from these summits.

Between these two mountains lie the Laghi delle Meraviglie, the Lakes of Wonders. The water from them and also from all the other regions of the figured rocks, flows down into the Roja. That from the Meraviglie passes the Val d'Inferno and Val Aurea to the mines of Tenda, and a little below is joined by the river from the Casterino valley and is then called the Beonia, which reaches the Roja at S. Dalmazzo. We must describe the ascent from this place. The path follows the right bank of the foaming river through beautiful chestnut woods for three quarters of an hour, and then by meadows gay with yellow tulips and Poet's Narcissus in the early summer Another three quarters up steeper slopes bring one to a group of cottages called I Conventi, with cultivated terraces, mulberry and walnut trees, mountain ashes and the wild *Prunus Brigantiaca,* Vill. Soon after Scotch firs with mistletoe on them and larches begin, and Monte Bego comes into sight. On reaching an elevation of 1335 m. at a spot called Le Mesce, the mingling or union of the waters, the Valley of Casterino opens out to the right. Here are many glacier-polished rocks. After another short ascent we reach Val Aurea, and in half an hour the argentiferous lead mines. These have many times changed hands, and have not been very prosperous on account of the expense of transport of the metal, but they are now, in 1912, worked by a Belgian company, which has built good lodgings for the miners and a little church, introduced new machinery, and erected overhead wires tor sending the minerals down to S. Dalmazzo. These mines are at 1509 m. From here there is a path on either side of the valley, and in half an hour we reach the entrance to Val Valauretta on the right, and cultivation ceases. The best path then continues on the right bank and passes the highest cattle sheds in the valley, I Tetti nuovi, where it is possible, but not advisable, to shelter for the night. Some way above the valley suddenly contracts, and there is a long and steep ascent with glaciated rocks and a few specimens of the Arolla pine, *Pinus Cembra L.* Up this the cattle do not go, only sheep and goats. The right of pasture above, though in Italian territory, belongs to the village of Saorgio in the Roja valley, now in France. On reaching the top of this ascent the valley again opens out into a wild and very desolate region called Val d'Inferno, the Valley of Hell. Here are most interesting "roches moutonnées," many of them crowned with large blocks of rock left by the retreating glaciers of old. We have sometimes asked shepherds how those blocks came to their present position. They had probably never noticed them before, but were much puzzled to give a reply. The path now crosses a little wooden bridge to the left bank of the stream, and a few metres farther on the rock figures begin, cut on dark purple schists. A small lake to the left, invisible from the path, is Lago Saorgino, but we soon reach two other larger ones, the lower and upper Laghi Lunghi. The scenery here is extremely grand. It is said that there were thick woods here two centuries and a half ago, but we think this statement must be an exaggerated one. Trees were, however, cut down at the beginning of the last century to furnish timber for new buildings at the mines, but no very large number would have been required, and the transport down the gorge would have been very difficult; but below it is evident that there has been a terrible slaughter of the larches in recent times, for as in Val Fontanalba, the bottoms of the trunks are stilll standing. Unhappily no more trees will grow in Val d'Inferno, for the goats, " the enemies of mankind," ravage the whole of the mountain sides and destroy everything. At present a few giant trunks lie rotting on the ground, and a few other stunted and dying ones are scattered over the desolate expanse of rock and scree. The mountains are of fine forms, and the rocks of a wonderful variety of colour, purple, green and yellow, and sometimes of almost a bright orange tint. In many parts they have been rounded, grooved and polished by the ice, and in others higher up, where they are of a more slaty nature, they are shattered into pinnacles and towers. The upper of the Laghi Lunghi is partly fed by water from the north flowing down the narrow Vallone delle Meraviglie. Ascending this on either side, in half an hour we reach the lower Lago delle Meraviglie, a small deep lake. On both sides of the valley and on the steep mountain sides above them are quantities of engraved rocks, also around and above the lake and beyond it. They extend high up the flank of Monte Bego, and as far as the lower of two small lakes, the upper Laghi delle Meraviglie, which lie under Gran Capelet. In the valley beyond the lower lake is also another small one, more really a pond formed by the melting snow, which may almost or perhaps quite disappear by the end of the summer, and near this are also a few figures. There are many other lakes in the neighbourhood, south and west of the Laghi Lunghi, the chief ones being the Lago del Carbone, Lago dell' Olio and the Laghi del Trem. At the west end and head of the upper of the Laghi Lunghi a path leads up the Arpeto valley to a pass, and over into the Gordolasca valley, and more to the south another one to the Passo del Trem under the Cima del Diavolo. On both sides of the Arpeto valley, near the Lago del Carbone and Laghi del Trem, and in a large high region above the crest west of the Vallone delle Meraviglie as far as the Arpeto ridge are also rock figures. Those near to the right bank of the Vallone and some above the lower lake seem to be the only ones that have been seen by others than ourselves. All this region we call the Meraviglie region. The lowest of the figured rocks are at about 2000 m., and the highest at about 2500 m. or a little more.

The second region of the engravings may be reached by continuing up the valley beyond the lower Lago delle Meraviglie, mounting the steep ascent at the head of it to the Col or Baissa di Valmasca and descending to the highest of the Valmasca lakes, the Lago Soprano del Basto. Basto means a pack-saddle, and the name is given to the three large Valmasca lakes on account of the rounded ice-worn rock-wall which divides them from the Val Valmasca proper. Half way between the Col and the upper lake are a few figures. They are not easily found, and are very much worn on highly disintegrated rock, and we have not discovered anything there really worth seeing. It is better, however, if desired, to reach this locality by another route to be described presently.

The third region is that of Val Valauretta. The figures there can hardly be said to be in the valley so named, but are under the eastern cliffs of Monte Bego. In the lower part of this region there is good pasture under the larch trees, but in the upper part where are the figures there is only a wilderness of rocks. These figures may be reached from the Miniera valley or equally well from Val Casterino by way of Val Fontanalba.

The fourth region is the vast one in and above the Val Fontanalba, the Fontanalba region. Val Casterino, as we have said, joins the Miniera valley some way below the mines. If we ascend the valley by the right bank, we soon cross a little bridge where there is a magnificent waterfall and some interesting 'giant's caldrons'. We then mount rapidly and presently reach some pleasant level meadows with firs and larches. On the right are the precipitous limestone cliffs below Monte Urno, in which are a good many small grottoes, and the steep hillsides covered with *Pinus silvestris, P. montana,* a few *P. Cembra* and larches. In the distance to the north are seen the summits of Peirafica 2661 m. and Rocca dell'Abisso 2735 m. In another half hour we reach a group of houses where till lately stood the ruined chapel of S. Maria Maddalena. A century ago, or perhaps more, for " a hundred years ago " is always the answer we receive when asking questions of the peasants, mass used to be said there regularly. In those days the valley was more thickly populated in the summer months, and the hillsides more cultivated. The people of Tenda used to grow rye, potatoes, and perhaps a little wheat and buckwheat, and mow their hay in the few grassy fields along the river banks. The abandoned terraces to be seen everywhere, the remains of cottages, and the now broken-down walls of sheds attest that the valley was once more inhabited, but for a long time Nice, Mentone, Bordighera, San Remo and other towns on the coast have attracted the people of Tenda and other villages near. Many have become accustomed to go down to the seacoast to work from autumn to spring, only coming back into the mountains for a summer holiday, and many have set up business on the seaboard and altogether given up an agricultural life. The old chapel, lately altered and enlarged, is now called the Villa di S. Maria Maddalena, where rooms are sometimes let to visitors and sportsmen, and where soldiers of the Alpine regiments or the Mountain Artillery, who often camp for a few days in the valley, or the miners from an hour away come to drink on their holidays. There are generally a few cattle in the valley, but the large herds of white cows which come from Saluzzo in June, by a three days' march, soon go up to higher regions. Where their pasture ceases are sheep and goats, but not in great numbers. Sometimes all the pastures are not let, and the palmy days of the shepherds seem to be over.

S. Maria Maddalena is at 1550 m. From this centre the figures in Val Fontanalba and in the Valauretta region may be easily reached, but over four hours of steady walking are required to arrive at the L. delle Meraviglie by either of the direct routes. The one by the mines has been described; the other is by the Fontanalba valley and the Baissa di Valmasca. A little below S. M. Maddalena the stream from Val Fontanalba joins the Casterino river. The Fontanalba valley is not seen from below, being hidden by the steep hillside. The lower part of its stream falls rapidly in a series of cascades down a narrow ravine, but on ascending by a path on either side of it for about twenty minutes we come to open meadows with larch woods above, and at the head of the valley see the triangular top and serrated crest of Monte Bego. On the left are the limestone crags of the Ciavraireu ridge, rich in plants; on the right is the crest between Val Fontanalba and Val Valmasca, with the conspicuous summits of Monte Paracuerta 2386 m. and M. Santa Maria 2782 m. The path on the left bank passes the lower and middle cattlesheds, called Vastere or Margherie, and reaches the third and highest one just above the little green lake Lago Verde. The path up the right bank passes a copious spring, the water from which falls down in a white cascade to the river below, and from which the valley probably derives its name, and eventually reaches the lower end of Lago Verde. This is the more beautiful walk of the two. Lago Verde is an enchanting spot, surrounded by larches and immense blocks of rock, and patches of grass covered with alpine flowers.

There are figured rocks high up on the hillside above the left bank of the river, and on the eastern slopes of a great buttress which runs north and south across the valley below the lake, but they begin in greater numbers near the lake and upper Margheria, are scattered over all the region of glaciated rocks to the north and northwest, and extend as far as the scree under Monte Bego.

At the head of the Fontanalba valley a low pass leads over to the Valauretta figures just under Monte Bego, and another pass to the north, the Baissa di Fontanalba, leads down to those by the Lago Soprano del Basto. From the Baissa di Fontanalba one may also cross pretty directly to the Baissa di Valmasca, and descend to the Meraviglie valley. There is also a pass between the cliffs to the south of Lago Verde by which one may reach the Valauretta region. 'The head of the Lago Soprano del Basto may also be reached by going up the Valmasca valley, which is the continuation of Val Casterino. One may pursue the valley till one reaches a small deep lake under the precipices of M. S. Maria, and then descend to the great lake, or on reaching the highest cattleshed in the valley ascend to the lower of the three Valmasca lakes north of the Basto, and find a path to the left of them. This is perhaps the most beautiful of the not very long excursions from Val Casterino, for on the north side of the lakes are the fine peaks of Cima di Lusiera 2897 m. and Monte Ciaminejas 2913 m., with Gran Capelet and many other high peaks beyond them.

The fifth region where we have discovered a few figured rocks is below Col Sabbione, above the Casterino valley. This may be reached by going up the valley on the left bank till we come to the bottom of the Valmasca gorge, and crossing over a gulley mount the hillside towards the Col, a little below which will be seen some smoothish rock surfaces. This is a walk of about two hours from S. M. Maddalena.

From the above descriptions it will be seen that if persons who wish to study the prehistoric rock-engravings do not care to camp out in the higher regions, they will do well to sleep at the Miniera for excursions to the Meraviglie and Valauretta regions, and in Val Casterino for those to Val Fontanalba. A mule can be taken as far as the bottom of the Vallone delle Meraviglie, some distance up Valauretta, and a long way beyond Lago Verde in the Fontanalba region to the slopes under the summit of M. S. Maria. The times required for reaching the figured rocks are approximately,

From the Miniera to Lago delle Meraviglie 3 hours.

    „   „   „   „ Valauretta rocks $2\,^{1}/_{2}$ - 3 „

    „   „   „   „ Lago Verde $2\,^{1}/_{2}$ - 3 „

From S. M. Maddalena to Lago delle Meraviglie 4 hours.

    „ „ „   „   „ Lago Verde 1 hour 40 min.

    „ „ „   „   „ Valauretta rocks 3 hours.

It may be well to state that all the regions of the rock figures lie within the military district of Tenda, which bristles with military roads, forts and batteries, and that permission should be obtained to photograph for scientific purposes. Not uncommonly cameras are sequestrated at Tenda or San Dalmazzo. In 1897 and 1898 this rule was not in force, and we were able to photograph freely, but in later years we have each season obtained a fresh permission to do so.

Val Casterino is a very good centre for many interesting excursions besides those to the rock figures. The scenery in the valley itself is not remarkable, but there are fine views from all the surrounding heights. The summit of Monte Ciagiore, the highest point of the limestone ridge on the east, 2294 m., may be climbed in two hours. From the top we look down into the Roja valley, and see the little station of Vievola at our feet, and the entrances both by road and rail into the tunnels under the Col di Tenda. North and west are many of the high peaks of the Maritime Alps. Not far off is the central fort of the Col di Tenda, and other forts from which the large guns sometimes practise across the mountains in August. Beyond them one sees the military road which winds along the crest of the chain between Liguria and Piedmont, and which ends at the forts of Nava on the pass from Albenga to Ormea. To the west and south are fine views of the lower mountains down to the sea. About three kilometres north of S. M. Maddalena is the deep gorge leading into Val Valmasca with its grand peaks. Besides the three Valmasca lakes the large Lago Agnel is well worth a visit, and with a guide the summit of Monte Clapier, 3046 m. may be ascended, and the hotel at the Madonna delle Finestre be reached in the evening. The largest glacier in the Maritime Alps lies under the precipices of Monte Clapier. Monte Santa Maria, north of Val Fontanalba, is an easy four hours' walk. From the top one looks down on the Valmasca lakes, and sees some of the plains of Piedmont and the ranges of the Alps far away. From here Monte Rosa is hidden, but is seen from a small summit lower down on the crest, to which the Italian Alpine Club has politely given the name Cima Bicknell. The finest view of all is from the summit of the Rocca dell'Abisso, a four hours' climb of no difficulty. As it is on the crest of the central chain there is nothing to hide the view of the whole range of mountains from Monte Viso to Monte Rosa and beyond. Mont Blanc also may easily be distinguished.

The geology of all this region is of great interest, as may be seen from the study of Professor Sacco's work, *Il Gruppo dell'Argentera*, and from the maps which accompany it. The upper part of the Valmasca valley and a little of the Fontanalba one near the Baissa di Fontanalba are of gneiss, as are the high mountains north of the Valmasca lakes. Rocca dell'Abisso, Monte Bego, M. S. Maria, Gran Capelet and all the regions of the rock figures are anagenite, a breccia consisting of fragments of quartz with siliceous and talcose cement, with bands of quartz and schists. In some parts the breccia is a veritable pudding stone, composed of large pieces of differently coloured stones. The anagenite and schists vary greatly in colour. The anagenite is as a rule greyish, but there are, especially in the Meraviglie region, strata of a dark purple colour. These belong to the Permo-trias series. The cliffs high up on both sides of Val Casterino and on the south of Val Fontanalba, of the middle and upper Trias, are limestone. The summits of Ciavraireu, Monte Urno, Monte Agnellino and Monte Paracuerta are of Jurassic limestone. Great glaciers must at one time have filled the Valmasca, Fontanalba, Casterino and Miniera valleys, and descended to San Dalmazzo, where may be seen still the remains of the terminal moraine. In all these valleys are signs of the ice work, especially below and above the Miniera, in the Val d'Inferno and in all the Valmasca valley, and all the rock

engravings have been cut upon surfaces which have been polished
by the glaciers.

There are a good many plants in the neighbourhood peculiar to
the Maritime Alps, but the flora is not so rich as it would be if
there were more calcareous rock. On this latter are to be found
*Alyssum halimifolium L., Saxifraga diapensioides Bell., Asperula
hexaphylla All., Phyteuma cordata Balb., Pedicularis Allionii Rchb.,
Micromeria Piperella Benth.* Others are *Viola nummularifolia All.,
Silene cordifolia All., Silene Campanula P., Galium Tendae All.,
Senecio Balbisianus D. C., Campanula stenocodon B. R., Fritillaria
Burnati and F. Moggridgei.* Edelweiss, the much overrated flower,
called in Italy Stella d'Italia, to gather which so many lose their
lives in Switzerland and elsewhere, is the commonest of common
plants on the limestone. The glory of the Maritime Alps, *Saxifraga
florulenta Mor.* is to be found on vertical cliffs in Val Fontanalba
and in Val Valmasca, the latter being the habitat farthest east at
present known.

Chamois abound in this region. In the early part of the summer we often see them quite low down, but when the valleys
become more populated, and particularly if any soldiers come to
shoot, they are frightened away; but later on we often come across
them higher up, and as they know that we are not sportsmen,
and would much rather make friends with them than shoot them,
they do not seem to be afraid of us, and not unfrequently come
quite close to us. We often hear the sound of falling stones which
they have dislodged, and then catch sight of a herd crossing the
scree or the snow slopes, and sometimes running up and down
after one another for all the world like children at play. They
generally stop and watch us as we watch them, and then suddenly
the leader starts off and the rest follow, lightly galloping and
leaping as they only can from rock to rock, and passing with
ease and rapidity over the places where we can only walk with
the greatest care and with wearisome slowness. Once we came
up to a herd of goats near which a number of chamois were
quietly feeding, having no fear of their near relations, but when
they became aware of our presence they were alarmed and rushed
up to the top of some crags near and stood there in graceful

attitudes against the skyline. In 1897 we tried to bring up a little chamois whose mother had been shot during the close season by one of those sportsmen so-called, to whom no life is sacred. A goat came to give it milk twice a day, but though the little creature seemed very well for some time, and was quite tame, playing with us and running up and down the stairs after us, one day it was suddenly taken ill. Mr James Berry F. R. C. S. and Mrs Dickinson Berry M. D. used their united skill, in hopes of saving its life, but in half an hour it died, to our great sorrow. Other game is not very abundant. There are blackcock among the Rhododendron bushes, ptarmigan in the higher regions, and occasionally we see a hare, and more rarely squirrels and foxes. Marmots may be seen, or at least heard always in the higher valleys.

PLATE I.

1. The lower of the Laghi delle Meraviglie.

2. A schist rock in Val Fontanalba.

PLATE II.

Engraved rocks in Val Valauretta.

CHAPTER II.

Accounts of the Laghi delle Meraviglie and Val Fontanalba regions
by previous writers and visitors.

The first person, as far as we know, who wrote about the figured rocks was the historian Gioffredo, whose work *The History of the Maritime Alps,* appeared about the year 1650. This was printed at Turin in 1824. He had received his information about them from a certain Onorato Laurenti, the parish priest of Belvedere, which is a village in the Vesubie valley, now in French territory, and which may be reached by crossing the pass beyond the Laghi Lunghi, and descending the Gordolasca valley. We do not know if the priest had himself seen them, or if he had only heard of them from sportsmen or shepherds. The name Laghi delle Meraviglie was then known. Gioffredo says " The above mentioned lakes are called the Lakes of Marvels, because near them, to the wonder and amazement of beholders, are to be found various rocks of different colours, smooth and slippery, which are engraved with a thousand figures representing quadrupeds, birds, fish, mechanical, rural and military implements, with historical and fabulous events. And these rocks, notwithstanding the length of time, are not covered by bushes, which causes no little astonishment to the curious. Laurenti writes that among other things are to be seen the figures of shields, of the ancient Labarum with the eagle, and of other Roman ensigns upon long poles. From which it is to be believed that the figures were done many centuries ago, and that the authors of these spirited jokes were probably only shepherds and herdsmen who wished to while away their idle hours." (Pl. I-1).

From that date to 1821 these figures do not seem to have engaged anyone's attention. Then a Monsieur Fodéré wrote of them. After speaking of the long sojourn of the Carthaginian armies in Italy, he says " Nous avons le témoignage d' historiens dignes de foi, et des monuments qui attestent le passage des Carthaginois par les Alpes Maritimes, non par d'Annibal, mais des généraux qui sont venus après lui..... Ces Africains trouvèrent des amis parmi les Salyens et les Liguriens, lesquels s'unirent aux Insubriens pour grossir l'armée de Hamilcar, successeur d'Hasdrubal." Later he continues "Pour les monuments, il en existe un dans un petit vallon au bas du Col d'Enfer, pres des Lacs des Merveilles, dont je parlerai plus bas. Ce sont d'énormes pierres de taille détachées d'un rocher voisin, qu'on voit étendues à terre en grand nombre, et sur lesquelles sont gravés grossièrement, mais d'une manière encore visible, des chevaux, des tours, des chariots armés de faulx, des vaisseaux en forme de galères, des casques, des boucliers, des arcs, des piques et d'autres instruments de guerre, avec beaucoup d'écritures qui ne sont ni grecques, ni latines, ni arabes, et qu'on conjecture être des caractères puniques. Ces pierres paraissent avoir été préparées pour un monument qu'on n'a pas eu le temps d'élever." It is not likely that Monsieur Fodéré had been to see them. He would not have spoken of rocks prepared for a monument which, for want of time, was not erected, or conceived that anyone could ever have intended to erect a monument in such a place. He had probably only heard stories much the same as those related to Gioffredo, though the account and list of the marvels had considerably developed in a century and a half.

The eminent geographer Elisée Reclus next spoke of the rocks in 1864 in his *Villes d'Hiver*, pp, 373-374. He had not been there and merely says "Les petits Lacs des Merveilles..... doivent leur nom à des rochers de forme étrange, qui semblent avoir été sculptés de main d'homme. D'après Fodéré, on y verrait en effet, des inscriptions hieroglyphiques en langue inconnue. Les montagnards disent que ces rocs on été taillés par les soldats d'Annibal."

In 1868 Mr M. Moggridge F. G. S., an English botanist who had spent six winters at Mentone, and who had heard much of the ' Marvels' from the natives but who had not been able to go up into the high mountains in the winter time when the rocks are always covered by snow, determined to make a midsummer excursion. Accompanied by Herr Dieck, an able and intelligent Prussian naturalist and near relative of Count Bismarck, he ascended from San Dalmazzo to I Tetti Nuovi, and there erected some sort of shelter. On the following days, probably two, they visited the right bank of the Vallone delle Meraviglie and some of the hillside above it. Though provided with ample materials for taking rubbings, casts etc., the weather was so bad that little could be done by those methods. Mr. Moggridge therefore confined himself to the task of finding fresh subjects, while his companion made pencil drawings. He read a paper upon his researches in August of the same year at the International Prehistoric Congress in Norwich, which, together with four plates giving about 115 of the rock figures, was afterwards published. These two gentlemen seem to have seen more of the region than anyone else has done up to the time when we began our explorations. Their drawings give a very fair idea of the forms of many of the figures, though some are inaccurate. Mr Moggridge says " The tradition of the country is that they were the work of Hannibal's soldiers, but I am bound to say that Hannibal, in that country, plays the same role as Cæsar, Oliver Cromwell, and his Satanic Majesty in England, to one or other of whom is popularly assigned the authorship of those things which cannot otherwise be accounted for.

In 1875 a Dr Henry of Nice was at Tenda, and made several excursions both to the Meraviglie region and to Val Fontanalba. He unfortunately had not heard of Mr Moggridge's excellent work, and the article which he wrote in 1877 for *La Société des Lettres etc. des Alpes Maritimes* was entitled *Ancien glacier metamorphosé en monuments Carthaginois*. He had read the work of Elisée Reclus and his mention of Fodéré, and as he had been informed by chamois hunters that there were rocks near the lake which could be easily cut, and was aware of the quarries in the Roja valley above and below San Dalmazzo, where the schists naturally flake into slabs and cubes, he thought that Fodéré had probably spoken of similar rocks, and he went off to the Meraviglie with his children in search of such. When he reached the Laghi Lunghi one of the children pointed out the smooth and polished surfaces, and the farther he proceeded the more clearly he saw the signs of ancient glacier work. The rocks were worn, polished, striated and channeled, and of all sorts of strange shapes. He then began to suspect that Fodéré's monument might only be these ice-shaped rocks, and this suspicion became a certainty when he reached the lower of the Laghi delle Meraviglie. He must have passed, on whichever side of the valley he ascended, within a metre of many rocks covered with figures but he did not see them. One of the children then pointed out a rock much in the form of a curule chair, and another with a rounded concavity like a niche for a statue. Farther on he noticed the grooves made by the action of water, resembling, he says, the worn bas-reliefs to be seen on ancient Greek and Egyptian monuments, and some of these, seen at a certain distance, seemed to represent warriors and horses and floating draperies with fringes at their lower borders. Near the pond higher up the valley he noticed huge blocks roughly resembling the forms of dromedaries and elephants, and still farther a rounded rock-tower with parallel horizontal grooves so regularly marked that they seemed to have been cut by human hands. He very rightly remarks. that it would have been impossible for Hannibal's soldiers, however numerous and laborious, even after many months' work, to have cut with the implements they possessed in those days, these rocks which extend for several kilometres. He was, however, still perplexed by Fodéré's words that there were characters which are neither Greek, nor Latin, nor Arabic, but which are conjectured to be Punic ones. But a second excursion into Val Fontanalba, where also he noticed the numerous traces of glacier action, explained to his entire satisfaction the strange statement. There one of the children discovered two very remarkable rocks — and we know them quite well — not far from one another, and quite unlike in form and structure to other rocks near. They were formed of prisms with triangular bases joining one another, alternately 'saillants et rentrants,' so as perfectly to represent cuneiform characters, and there seemed to him no longer any doubt that these rocks, seen from some distance, and in the place from which they had since fallen, might have been taken to be fragments of Punic or Carthaginian inscriptions. (Pl. I-2.). Unfortunately owing to the indisposition of one of the children who was the family artist, he was obliged to shorten the excursion without being able to make drawings of them. Dr Henry adds that Fodéré's hypothesis with regard to the Carthaginians is an impossible one, and that if the soldiers had been assisted by the Ligurians in their passage across the Alps, their friends would not have led them into side valleys which would bring them to a series of more difficult passes than those to the east, and which would not have taken them directly across the central chain into Italy.

All this is very amusing, but we regret that the doctor did not see the rock figures, and all the more because he has given us in the latter part of his article a very excellent description of the glacier work in the valleys below. Unfortunately the account of his observations has been used by others, and a recent writer on the Riviera has said " Recent investigations have unmistakably shown that these outlines left on the surface of the rock were formed by the flints which a glacier dragged with it as it progressed century after century down the valley." Mr Hugh Macmillan in the first edition of his book *The Riviera, 1885*, says, when speaking of the village of Castellar above Mentone, " On some of the alpine rocks of this region may be seen very curious sculptures called Meraviglie, which tradition assigns to the soldiers of Hannibal's army, but they are evidently prehistoric carvings, similar to those of North and South America, Australia and New Zealand." Why he puts the Meraviglie in the neighbourhood of Castellar it is difficult to say. However, in the last edition he has done away with the prehistoric carvings altogether, by adding that they are more probably " the runes or hieroglyphics made by the stones embedded in a glacier as it flowed slowly over the surface which itself had smoothed." But he has no doubt about Hannibal, for he says that he marched up the Roja in his famous passage over the Alps from the south of Gaul into upper Italy, and that the memory of the great Carthaginian general is still engraved upon the traditions of the neighbourhood, and the peasants often speak of the wonderful sight of the swarthy African legions thundering past in the days of their remote ancestors.

In the same .year, 1877, when Dr Henry's account was published, the eminent French scientist Monsieur Emile Rivière, was sent by his government to study the Meraviglie inscriptions. He and his companion M. de Vesly spent twelve days encamped in the Vallone at an elevation 2200 m., and a most valuable paper was read by him the year following at the Paris Congress of the Association Française pour l'Avancement des Sciences. He made 408 squeezes, and fifty of these, copied and reduced by means of a pantograph with the most scrupulous exactitude, were published with his pamphlet and leave nothing to be desired. We only regret that he did not reproduce them all, as we should then probably know exactly where he had been. As it is, there seem to be a few figures which we do not appear to have found. He says that he found about fifty surfaces more or less covered with figures in and just above the Vallone for a length of two kilometres, that is from the bottom of the valley to some little distance above the lower lake. All the figures which he has reproduced with few exceptions we know well, and are not at a greater altitude, but he says that they reach to an altitude of nearly 2600 m. This must surely be an error, as Passo Arpeto above the Gordolasca valley is only 2563 m., and neither there nor at that height on the sides of Monte Bego have we seen figures. M. Rivière did not look at any rocks on the left bank of the Vallone. One of his guides or porters said that he knew of other figures some way off, but the approach of a storm and want of time did not allow him to proceed farther. The rocks which he found presenting the greatest number of engravings were in a defile near and above the lower lake. Of his interpretations of the meaning and authorship of the engravings we shall speak later.

On the evening that M. Rivière returned to San Dalmazzo, Monsieur Léon Clugnet of Lyon arrived there, and the next morning went up to the Vallone and lower lake, returning to S. Dalmazzo the same evening. But the day following he went again, and climbed up above the lake, to try and find other figures.

He seems to have considered that the rocks with polished surfaces were very rare except on the right bank of the Vallone, and that the engraved figures did not exist anywhere else; consequently all those on the opposite side of the valley were unknown to him, but he evidently went to the higher Meraviglie lake, and to the great yellow rock waves under the Rocca delle Meraviglie, as we know from some of his 150 drawings, and from the excellent map which accompanies them. These, with an account of his excursions, were published the same year. We cannot but admire M. Clugnet's pluck in making two arduous ascents on two consecutive days, but it is evident that he was able to spend very little time there, and M. Rivière is the only visitor who has made continuous observations and really accurate drawings. M. Clugnet thought that the rock engravings were the work of shepherds in their hours of repose. He believed that the figures of weapons dated from a time when the tribes in the mountains did not know the use of metals; their massive handles and broad blades seemed to show that they indicated weapons of stone. He says that the figures had probably been cut by stone implements, and that experiments made in the Saint Germain Museum had proved that flint implements were much better adapted to this sort of work than those of bronze or iron

The next year, 1878, M. Edmond Blanc, librarian at Nice, visited the Meraviglie in the month of May, at which time there must have been an immense quantity of snow near the lake, but with the help of M. Clugnet's map he had no difficulty in finding figures on the right bank of the Vallone. He was much impressed by the wild and rugged region, the naked rocks of fantastic shapes, the desolate valleys and frowning peaks. He says " It is impossible to picture to oneself anything more melancholy than this region. The lakes, reflecting the colour of the surrounding rocks, have a black colour, which along with the absolute stillness of their surfaces unruffled by any breeze, make them look like a mass of pitch. The summits of Monte Bego, Capelet, and the Cima del Diavolo, with their bare sides, horribly torn by avalanches, seem to be immense skeletons of infernal beings. A deadly silence reigns there, and if the tourist speaks out loud to give life to this fearful solitude; no echo responds. One would say that the waves of sound cannot travel in such a depressing environment."

M. Blanc seemed to think that at an altitude of 2300 m. there is no vegetation except that of lichens and mosses, and consequently that no shepherds ever passed or would pass there unless on their way from one valley to another where pasture might be found. We must admit that there is very little grass even of coarse kinds in the Vallone and near the upper lakes; nevertheless in summer there is sufficient fodder even there for sheep and goats, and they go up to the top of Monte Bego and to the Passo Arpeto; and though one cannot expect to see flowers in May where the snow has hardly melted, they are abundant all through the summer even in the crevices of the rocks, and late in September we have seen the summit of the Cima del Diavolo a veritable flower garden. Another remark is unfortunate. M. Blanc says "Why are there no figures on the glaciated rocks in the beautiful Fontanalba valley, and why should shepherds have engraved pictures of instruments for hunting and fishing, and none of houses, ploughs etc. ?" He did not know that Val Fontanalba and the Meraviglie region are both full of figures of ploughs, and, as we believe, especially in the former place, of those of habitations also. M. Blanc was impressed by the names of the surrounding mountains, Val d'Inferno, the valley of hell; Cima del Diavolo, the devil's peak; Monte Macruera, the lean, sterile, scraggy mountain; Monte Bego, a name possibly derived from the Celtic word Beg, meaning bad, and Val Valmasca, the valley of the witches; and so he came to the conclusion that these regions were in very ancient times the centre of worship paid to an unknown terrible divinity, and that hunters came there to gain his favour, or to thank him for their success in the chase and to picture on the rocks the game they had killed, and the weapons and other things which had enabled them to do so. M. Blanc published drawings of 36 figures, and gave an excellent description of them.

In 1880 M. Molon published his *Preistorici e Contemporanei* at Milan, and referred to the Meraviglie, giving a selection of 54 figures copied from M. Clugnet's plates. After mentioning various kinds of figures, among which he saw characteristic representations of stags, elks, aurochs and wild boars, he says that they were probably executed in the period of transition between the end of the Stone Age and beginning of the Bronze Age. He had not visited the Meraviglie. He is the first person, as far as we know, who mentioned Val Fontanalba. He says "Tradition relates that above Breglio, in the province of Nice, and near the Fontana Alba, are inscribed upon the rocks signs of a primitive language," and he has no doubt that those in the Meraviglie region are such, together with "hieroglyphics and perhaps conventional signs of a rudimentary alphabet."

In 1884 papers appeared in the *Bollettino del Club Alpino* by Signor S. Navello, whose illustrations and more important remarks are copied from M. Clugnet's work, and by Signor A. F. Prato in the *Rivista Alpina Italiana*. The former, who had seen the rocks, ridicules M. Blanc's theories of the superstitious people and their divinity, and believes that the shepherds cut the figures in their hours of repose, and though admitting that the engravings are very ancient and prehistoric, seems to think that the people who made them were the direct ancestors of the present shepherds, for he finds that these have a special talent for cutting figures on their sticks and flutes, and that there is not a family in the neighbourhood which does not possess something decorated in the same manner.

Signor Prato, who had not seen the place, and only comments upon Signor Navello's paper, suggests that hunters cut the figures in memory of their deceased friends who had died there during their hunting excursions, and that all the figures had reference to the animals they sought for food, and to the weapons and instruments of the chase. As Signor Navello had observed that all the figures of animals' heads were represented without ears, he thought that the sculptors intended to represent skulls, the trophies of their expeditions.

We now come to the year 1885 when the late Professor Celesia of Genova published a pamphlet on the rock figures. He had not as yet seen them himself, but he made an earnest appeal to his fellow-countrymen to explore their own near mountains. He was perhaps thinking of M. Molon's words that M. Rivière, a Frenchman, who first explored the Ligurian caves near Mentone, and then the Meraviglie rocks, had won his scientific fame in Italy. The following 7th of August he arrived at Tenda, but the friends who had been waiting for him had already been to the Meraviglie, but they had been driven away by a storm and did. not desire to make a second ascent. They returned home, leaving the professor at Tenda. Several times he started to reach the Val d'Inferno, but each time the thick mists ahead, the sound of thunder, and the swollen waters of the Beonia indicated that it was useless to proceed. He was about to give up the enterprise altogether, when the thought struck him that he might perhaps be able to explore other neighbouring valleys, and especially that of Fontanalba, in which he had been told there were similar figures. It seems strange, with the reputation which the Meraviglie lakes have so long enjoyed, that this second region was not known earlier; but it is certain that such things are of very little interest to the people of the neighbourhood. Val Fontanalba has probably never been visited by tourists, as it ends at the foot of the precipices of Monte Bego, whereas the path to the well-known Passo del Trem or Passo Arpeto, by one of which the priest Laurenti probably crossed from Belvedere — that is, if he himself had ever been to the Meraviglie — leads close to the lowest of the most usually known engraved rocks. Chamois hunters of old, as today, would have gone to the Meraviglie region or to Val Valmasca, and all modern climbers ascend Monte Bego or the high mountains above the Valmasca lakes, without passing through Val Fontanalba. The upper part of this valley has till lately been practically unknown except to the few shepherds and goatherds who have rented the scanty pasture there. The professor must have attempted the Val della Miniera on the 8th and 9th of August, as he says 'several times'; but anyhow on the night of the 9th, with the communal schoolmaster of Tenda Sig. Degiovanni, Prof. Bacchialoni and two guides, he started, reached S. M. Maddalena in Val Casterino, and began to ascend Val Fontanalba. They climbed some of the hillsides above the valley, where there was no vegetation, and there attentively examined all the rocks without discovering anything, but at last arrived, almost without hope of success, at Lago Verde. Around this they searched in vain, and then mounted to the sheds of the upper Vastera, where by good luck they fell in with two young goatherds who knew some of the figured rocks, and offered to guide them. Some of these were close to the sheds, others not far off, and some a good deal higher up just above the Valletta di Santa Maria at about 2500 m. It is difficult to understand exactly what happened, but it seems that the two friends drew at least 59 figures, and that Prof. Bacchialoni returned several times 'on successive days. Anyhow more than 70 figures together with a report of the excursion were published in the official bulletin of the Minister of Public Instruction. The visits were short and hurried, some of the drawings fairly accurate, others not so. We know quite well many of the rocks they visited, but wonder they did not copy more of the figures on those very rocks, where are representations of weapons, a man holding an implement, and many other forms quite different to those given. They may have seen other figured rocks which we have not found, as they give some figures which we do not recognize. Professor Celesia's paper is chiefly a treatise on the Phoenicians, whom he considers to have been the authors of the engravings. He sees representations of " the heads of ruminants, of snails, serpents, skins of animals, nets, oval and rectangular figures, diverse forms of weapons, tools altogether primaeval or unknown, some figures of men in strange attitudes, and several others bearing a distant resemblance to those already known in the Val d'Inferno." He was the first to discover the figure which is undoubtedly that of a man holding the handle of a plough to which two bullocks are yoked; this he calls "the figure of a man with uplifted arms, and perhaps expresses the idea of an offering to some tutelar divinity" (Pl. III.2 and Pl. XXVI).

After this visit Prof Celesia was unable to return, though he had hoped to do so. Indeed he died only a few months later, and we fear that his last illness dated from that memorable excursion.

This is all that has been written about Val Fontanalba till lately, and the region was forgotten and unvisited till we ourselves in 1897, twelve years later, went to spend the summer in Val Casterino.

We have given a somewhat long account of the work of our predecessors merely to show how very little had really been seen of that vast region, and in order to point out how rash it is to publish accounts and form theories about anything hastily. Mr Moggridge failed to do much owing to the stormy weather; M. Rivière only visited a small part of the Vallone delle Meraviglie; Dr Henry found nothing except the glaciated rocks; M. Clugnet, M. Blanc and Signor Navello all followed the same route and saw the same rocks, and only Prof. Celesia paid one hurried visit to Val Fontanalba. We must therefore give, as briefly as possible, an account of our whole work there up to the present time, but we are fully aware that if scientific men had had our opportunities, they would probably have made more important discoveries. They would have known where best to look for traces of the habitations or burial places of the prehistoric sculptors, and might have found what we have failed to do, and shed more light upon their mysterious work. We are only the collectors of facts, and must leave to others the task of studying them more profoundly.

CHAPTER III.

The Story of our own Explorations.

Soon after coming to winter on the Riviera in 1879 I heard of the Meraviglie, and two years later walked up there from San Dalmazzo with friends, returning the same evening. It was in the early days of June, and there was so much snow upon the rocks and round the lake, which was itself almost covered with it, that we saw very little. In September of 1885 I went there again, having slept at the Miniera. This time I was able to explore more fully, saw figures on both sides of the Vallone and lake, and made about 50 drawings in my sketch-book. In 1897 I heard that a house in Val Casterino, belonging to Signor Pellegrino of Tenda, was to be let, and I took it for the summer, partly with the intention of botanizing, but partly with that of seeing more of the rock figures, which had from the first greatly fascinated me. Signor Luigi Pollini came up with me and has been my companion and helper ever since. About the end of June I wrote to the Secretary of the Italian Alpine Club to ask if he could give me any information about works already published on the Meraviglie, and he referred me to Dr Fritz Mader, an Associate who had a thorough knowledge of the Maritime Alps, and who spent his summers in Tenda. It was then, through the full and courteous reply to a letter which I wrote to Dr Mader, that we first heard of there being engravings in the valley near us, and we immediately went up to search for ourselves. I had, only a few weeks previously, been up the Val Fontanalba for the first time with a nephew. The sight of some chamois on the snow slopes in the distance enticed us on, and when near the foot of Monte Bego we decided to come back another way crossing over the rocks to the foot of M. Santa Maria. We passed over a number of smooth yellow rocks, and I

remember observing that they were exactly like those at the Meraviglie, but intent on looking for plants and choosing as far as possible the grassy strips rather than the rocks, I noticed no figures,
though I now know that I must have passed quite close to many
of the most decorated surfaces and probably even upon some of
the engraved ones. If, however, we had lit upon some of those of
a brilliant red colour, it would have been impossible not to have
descried some figures. On this second excursion we at once discovered a number of them a little way beyond Lago Verde. After
this we dedicated as much of our time as possible to explorations
until we returned to the coast in September. At first we made
some 450 small drawings, but seeing that they were far from
satisfactory, we procured large sheets of paper from Tenda and
began to take pencil rubbings. We made about 211 of these in 13
long days, and we also went twice to the Meraviglie. Our friend
Signor Benigni, an able photographer at Bordighera, kindly came
up and took some excellent pictures for us, of which a few are
here reproduced.

The next year we again went to Val Casterino in August,
remaining three weeks, and with better paper and heelball did
better work, bringing home 538 rubbings in our twelve visits, and
about a hundred photographs taken with small Kodak and Frena
Cameras. We carried away two small pieces of detached rock,
each with a horned figure upon it, one of which we kept for our
little local museum in Bordighera, and the other we sent to the
British Museum, where it is now exhibited in the same case with
other Italian prehistoric objects. We also sent rubbings to London,
to Prof. Issel of Genoa, Prof. Pigorini of Rome, and Dr. Lissauer of
Berlin. In that summer we discovered figures on the rocks above the
upper Lago del Basto, probably in the place where it had been report-
ed to Prof. Celesia and Dr Mader that they existed, for we have
often searched in other parts of the valley but in vain. We went twice
into Val Valauretta and examined the more promising yellow surfaces there, but could not detect any signs of human workmanship.

In the winter of 1897 I read a short paper before the members
of the Società Ligustica in Genoa, and in 1898 wrote another one
for their bulletin, about the rock figures.

After this we spent two summers elsewhere, having the idea that we were well acquainted with these regions and with the rock engravings, but we were mistaken, and happily we were always haunted by the thoughts of our prehistoric friends who seemed to be calling us back again, and so in 1901, hearing that Signor Pellegrino had not let his house, we determined to spend another summer there. This turned out most successfully, as we finally discovered figures in Val Valauretta, which, as far as we had ascertained had never been seen there. (Pl. II.) We have since been told that some of these were also known to the shepherds, though they do not seem to have ever spoken of them, but we are never sure if the figures which they profess to know are really the prehistoric ones, or merely the names and scratches cut by their friends. In previous years we had scarcely looked at any rocks in Val Fontanalba which had no coloured and polished surface, but this year we learnt that there are numberless ones from which the colour has long worn off, but on which the figures are still though less clearly visible. Neither had we dreamed before of exploring the long slopes of the mountain side west of the Lago di Paracuerta, which appear and are so rugged and grey, but where we have now discovered so much. We paid two visits to the Meraviglie, and renewed our acquaintance with the Lago del Basto. We spent 20 days in Val Fontanalba, making nearly 700 rubbings, including duplicates, and over 100 squeezes. We found two more detached pieces of rock with figures, one of which we gave to Prof. Issel for his Genoa museum, and another to Dr L. Capitan for that of anthropology in Paris, and to both of them a collection of rubbings and squeezes. In 1901 an excellent article on the Laghi delle Meraviglie and Val Fontanalba, written by Dr Mader, appeared in the Review of the Italian Alpine Club, and a still more valuable one by Prof. Issel in the Bollettino di Paleontologia Italiana, to which we shall refer later.

The summer of 1902 saw us again in Casterino, where we had the pleasure of a visit from Prof F. Sacco of Turin, and Prof. Issel and his son Dr R. Issel, also from the learned mineralogist Captain A. Pelloux. In that year we discovered for the first time that there are many purple rocks in tle valley immediately beyond

Lago Verde with figures on them and which have apparently never had any of the smooth yellow coating. We also found figures in many new places including some in Val Valauretta cut upon purple rocks. We began copying on large sheets of paper some of the largest figures and also groups of them as they are placed on the rocks. We mounted for the first time to the crest of the ridge above the right bank of the Vallone delle Meraviglie, and learnt that beyond it to the west are two other valleys parallel with the Vallone, filled with smooth coloured rocks, and that there are figures in all this hitherto unexplored region. We also saw for the first time figures in the neighbourhood of the Laghi Lunghi upon the smoother purple rocks, and in the valley leading to the Cima del Diavolo.

The following year we heard with dismay that Signor Pellegrino had sold his house, and as there was no other abode in the valley where it would be possible to make a lengthy stay with any sort of comfort, we feared that our work was over. But we soon came to the decision that we must build a cottage for the summer, and in 1904 this was settled. We bought pine trees from a man in the valley, ordered lime to be made, and engaged a builder of Tenda to carry out the excellent plan which Mr Robert Mac Donald, son of Dr George Mac Donald, had kindly made for us. Sig. Pellegrino undertook to superintend the building operations, but these were not easy in a mountain valley four hours away from a town. Workmen did not care to come up to such a dull place. Everything except stone, lime, and sand had to be brought by mules from Tenda and expenses were at least doubled. However in July, 1905, the cottage was begun on a charming site just above the bottom of the Fontanalba stream, with a small piece of flat land round it for a vegetable garden, and all the rest a wilderness of old moraine boulders and fallen rocks. We spent a few weeks there to see the work well started, and came up again late in the autumn when the cottage was completed, just in time before the heavy falls of snow. We were only able to go four times to the Fontanalba rocks and spent one day at the Meraviglie.

The next year we went up as early as possible in June. A cemented terrace was made in front of the house, a carpenter on the spot

made us rough tables, cupboards and shelves, and we took up
our abode in Casa Fontanalba. Very much time was spent during
the whole summer in clearing away the lime and rubbish left by
the builders, in painting and decorating our walls, in endeavouring
to cultivate small patches of soil between the rocks, in making a
channel through the property to divert water from the river above
us so that it should pass close to the house, and in engineering
paths, bridges etc. Nevertheless we worked hard in the rock regions, discovered abundant figures near the Lago del Carbone in
the Meraviglie region, and also low down near our camping ground
by the Laghi Lunghi, and climbed higher up the steep slopes of
Monte Bego than we had ever been before with great success,
finding some figures at an elevation of over 2500 m.

Since then we have spent every summer in our cottage, each
year finding more figured rocks or descrying new figures on those
already known, and each year in August or September, we have
spent three days in the Meraviglie region, sleeping in our tent
near a great rock shelter close to the lower of the Laghi Lunghi.
This spot is easily found, as the path passes close by, and nearly
every year soldiers of the Alpine regiments or the Mountain Artillery encamp there. The officers have sometimes told us that they
had had no time to go to the Meraviglie lake and see the figures,
but on the rocks within a few metres of their tents there are
numbers of them, though we believe that noone whose eyes were
not trained by long experience as are ours would be likely to notice them, as they are all cut on dark surfaces, and cannot be
seen by anyone who is not scrutinizing the rock quite closely, for
at a distance of a metre or two they are quite invisible even to
ourselves. An account of these two years' work was given in the
Ligurian Society's Bulletin.

In the two years following, 1907 and 1908, we paid greater
attention to the figures of which only a part could just be seen
above ground, and disinterred a great number of them. Some of
these have been covered up to a depth of 30-50 cm. We also settled to try and draw everything so as to make a complete collection
and obtain an approximate idea of the whole number of figures,
and of the various types. We had only before copied the more

conspicuous and interesting ones, but now regret that we did not draw everything from the beginning, for we are often not sure what we have drawn before, and not wishing to copy the same figures again, unless for friends who ask for some, we have to spend much time in consulting our notes, and also from time to time neglect to copy figures because we erroneously believe that we have done so before. An account of these two years' work was published as before.

In 1909, and 1910, we made the discovery of figures of particular interest in the Fontanalba and Meraviglie regions, of which we have given some account in *La Revue Préhistorique* of April 1911, and also another of still greater importance. This was that there are about twenty figures on some smoothish surfaces below the path leading to Col Sabbione, overlooking the left bank of Val Càsterino at a height of about 2100 m.

In 1911 we worked diligently as before, finding very little new in Val Fontanalba, but a good deal near the Laghi Lunghi, some of the figures being of quite a new type, and others in a place where we had never thought of looking as it seemed so very unlikely that there could be anything there.

In this last year we did very little in Val Fontanalba. Never had we seen so much snow there before, and even at the end of August very many of the best surfaces were still partly covered by it.

Our explorations in the Fontanalba region are now nearly at an end, though there is no doubt that there are still more figures to be found or copied, and a good many more at the Meraviglie. There are very many more figures on the slopes above the head of the upper Laghi Lunghi where we have only been once, this last year, and from which we were driven away by a heavy storm.

The sum total of our work in as follows. We have spent the best part of twelve summers in these researches. We have passed 181 days in Val Fontanalba, and copied there about 7000 figures; 33 days at the Meraviglie and copied 4500 figures, and 5 in Valauretta where we have copied about 130 figures. We may therefore take it for certain that there are some 12000 figures in the whole region, probably more, for we know of many rocks which have evidently been engraved, but where nothing is now sufficiently clear to allow of its being copied. We must add that in August 1909 Professor Cartailhac paid us a visit, and was greatly interested in his long day's excursion in Val Fontanalba. He found the rocks much more wonderful and interesting than he had expected, and he said " It is a great mystery." Prof. Issel in his *Liguria Preistorica* (Genova 1903) has devoted a long chapter to them, the most important and comprehensive contribution to the subject yet written, and we shall presently avail ourselves largely of his learning and judgment.

CHAPTER IV.

Description of the Rock Engravings.

The schists upon which the figures are chiefly cut are of a very hard nature, and are for the most part of grey, greyish green or green colour, but some are purple or reddish purple. These schists are mixed with bands of anagenite and quartz. The green and most compact kind is extensively quarried near Tenda, and is known as Marmo or Pietra di Tenda. It is much used for building purposes, for steps, balconies, wall copings etc., also for basins, chimney-pieces, cemetery monuments, and more ornamental work in palaces and churches, but it is not capable of a very high polish. * The ancient sculptured façade of the parish church of Tenda is of this stone. In some places the schists are not compact but split into flakes, but the rock figures have with very few exceptions never been cut upon any of these. The surfaces mostly chosen by the sculptors have moreover been polished by glacier action, and have a thin coating of different colour, yellow, orange or red, which sometimes penetrates to a depth of five millimetres but generally less. These varieties of colour in the bands of schist, and also of the anagenite, which is grey or purple, greatly add to the beauty of the region, and especially in the neighbourhood of the Meraviglie lakes. Some of the rocks are extremely brilliant. The long banks of smooth rock with little grass terraces between them under the Rocca delle Meraviglie are of a tawny orange colour, and are most conspicuous from the Laghi Lunghi. These we have called the Rock Waves, as they somewhat resemble in form the long undulations which we see on our coast after a storm at sea. In the Fontanalba region there are surfaces of many shades.

---

* These schists form the subject of two very interesting pamphlets by A. Roccati:
  1. *La Pietra della Roja*. Perugia 1910.
  2. *Sopra alcuni schisti della Valle della Roja*. Roma 1910.

PLATE III.

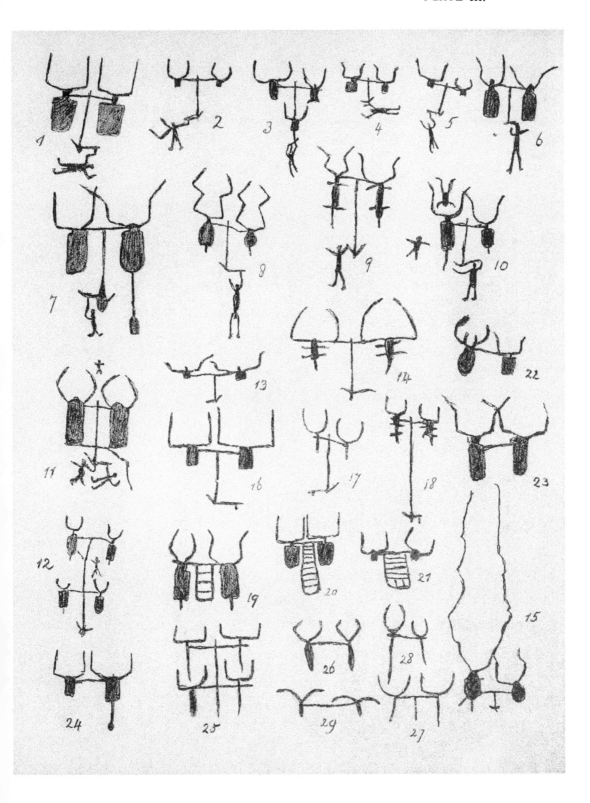

Ploughs with oxen and men. Oxen with plough and harrow.
Yoked horned figures.

of red. The colour of the great smooth surface under Monte Santa.
Maria may be distinctly seen from many kilometres away, and at
the head of the little gully are steep fan-shaped masses of rock
almost the colour of blood. Such coloured surfaces as these would
have tempted people in any part of the world to scratch, write,
or carve something, and to cut sufficiently deeply to destroy the
coloured coating so that their incisions would stand out in
strong relief. Some few figures are cut upon purple schists which
do not seem to have had any of this superficial colour, in consequence of which the figures are of the same colour as the surface,
and it is difficult to discern them. In some parts they have also been
cut upon the anagenite rocks of finer grain, never upon the coarser
sort of conglomerate; but the surface of these is not nearly as
smooth as that of the schists although glacier-polished. Perhaps
also a few figures have been cut upon gneiss near the head of
the Fontanalba valley, but of this we are not sure.

Many of these rocks appear at first sight to be as smooth as
polished marble, but they are not so. There are little holes and
cracks here and there as well as the fine striations made by the
ice, and we have found, when making squeezes by beating wet
paper with a brush, that many of these natural markings come out
too distinctly, and are almost or quite indistinguishable from parts
of the figures, especially when these latter are very shallow; and
it was partly for this reason that we gave up making squeezes,
and have for many years copied the figures with heelball, pressing
the paper into the engravings with one hand, and making the
outline of them with the heelball in the other, and afterwards rubbing
over the parts between the outlines with the heelball. With this
method we are thoroughly satisfied, though it is not possible tc
show all the spots which have been cut by mis-directed blows
making excrescences on the contour, or lying just outside it.

We have always endeavoured to copy the figures as accurately
as possible, without inventing anything to improve them, but we
often find it extremely difficult to be quite sure about their forms,
when there are many close together interlacing one another, or
where the rock is much worn, or has many natural cracks and
grooves. Some of our drawings may be, and probably are,

inaccurate, as are some of those which have been reproduced in other published plates. Very much depends upon the light or time of day when we copy them, for at midday in the summer time with the sun high in the sky, there is no shadow along the edges of the shallow engravings, and sometimes they are almost invisible then, although towards evening they become quite clear. It is particularly difficult to see the figures on rocks upon which water constantly flows after rain or for a long time in the summer from springs near, for both the rocks and figures become of a uniform blackish hue, and there is no sort of relief at any time. It therefore happens that in different years we have copied the same figures a little differently. Often also one of us discerns the outlines better than the other, and so our drawings do not quite agree. Sometimes friends with us have declared that our enthusiasm or imagination leads us to see things which are not really there, but we have been able to prove ourselves right by at once making a rough hasty rubbing of the figure and producing on the paper the distinct form which we said was there. Not seldom a figure seems very clear a little way off, but close by is less visible, but sometimes the reverse is the case, and only very close inspection enables us to see the true engraving. We have often thought that we had copied some horned figure entirely, and then a better light showed us that the horns were very much longer, or that there was a tail attached below, and sometimes we have made an addition which afterwards turned out to be a natural marking on the rock. Often we have drawn a figure without noticing that around it were a number of large spots, which were evidently intended to form part of the design; and over and over again we have passed rocks year after year, feeling quite sure there was nothing on them, until some exceptionally good light disclosed to our surprise a number of figures. Also we have often looked for a figure which we knew to be there, but on account of the bad light could not find it. Two of the most interesting rocks in Val Fontanalba we shall always remember, because though both of them were well known to us, we had seen no figures on them till, returning by the first one late one September evening, when the slightest depressions had some amount of shadow, we saw to our amazement that the rock was not only engraved, but that it was completely covered with figures like an elaborately patterned carpet. We called it *The September Rock*. The other one, standing alone on a slope close to a little goat track, we had often passed within a few metres; then one day when we went right up to it under very favourable conditions, we saw the four strange scalariform figures of a new type upon its four narrow smooth surfaces, and it received the name *Le Scale del Paradiso*. (Pl. XXI).

For the most part the figures have been cut on the living rock, but sometimes upon blocks which had previously fallen from their original position in the cliffs. A few of the figured surfaces are level with the ground, but the greater number at slight inclinations, and some on steeper rocks where it is difficult to stand or lie down without slipping. In some places are vertical surfaces of greenish hue, which have a special polish and seem exceptionally hard, but these have seldom any figures, as it is naturally more difficult to cut on a vertical surface than on an inclined one, especially low down near the ground. Where there are figures running some way underground, the soil must have risen nearly a metre since they were cut. This of course is one of the many proofs of their antiquity. The figures are never in a position where it would have been necessary to use a ladder. Many rocks seem to have been quite uninjured by frost or water, and are as fresh and smooth as when the ice left them. The sculptors chose their material very wisely, for though there are large tracts of smooth and yellow rock in all the region where no work has been done, and inferior surfaces have sometimes been selected, there are never or hardly ever any figures where the schists have become split up into flakes, however brightly coloured they may be. Some of the smooth surfaces in Val Fontanalba are of immense size, as much as 100 metres long and 20 metres wide. (Pl. XXXIII). We have never seen anything like them in other mountain regions, and indeed a great part of the Fontanalba figured rock region looks from the Lago Verde like a great but dirty glacier. (Pl. XXVIII). This part we call *The Central Mass,* and it is very conspicuous. It seems to flow down from the sky-line, between the steep slopes of M. Santa Maria on the north and the rough rock terraces on the south which are of a darker colour; but on exploring this central mass we find that there are little gullies here and there, or veritable ravines with steep cliffs bounding them, and lower rock walls innumerable in many places not easy to descend; and in crossing this glacier-like area one has to make many detours to avoid the awkward places. Here and there are little ponds and small tracts of grass and flowers, but the greater part is of rocks with only lines of grass between them, and the few sheep are never there, and the goats only pass over to better pasture.

The extreme distance between figures in the Meraviglie district north and south is about three kilometres, and between those east and west two and a half; in the Fontanalba valley the distance between those north and south is about one kilometre and a half, between those east and west two and a half; and the distance as the crow flies from the figures nearest Val Casterino to those near Passo Arpeto is about five kilometres. It will be seen then what a long time it takes to know the whole region thoroughly, and how difficult to locate the position of the more important rocks, and only after these many years have we come to know where many things are to be found or how best to reach them. The continual climbing up and down is fatiguing work, and every rock must be examined all round, for if one side of it be rough the other may be smooth and engraved, and one is never sure where one may not light upon something new. The figures have by no means been cut upon rocks where shepherds in old days would most probably have reposed while their flocks fed or rested. In the Vallone delle Meraviglie and around the lower lake there is very little pasture, whereas it is much better higher up towards the Passo Arpeto where there are few engravings. Round the Laghi Lunghi where grass is also most abundant the figures are few, and the same may be said about many parts of Val Fontanalba. At the foot of Monte Bego, a wilderness of scree and fallen rocks, and where snow rests very late in the year, are many figures, whereas in some places where there is much pasture and beautifully prepared rock surface there are none. Some places are very rich in figures; they are to be found close together on all

PLATE IV.

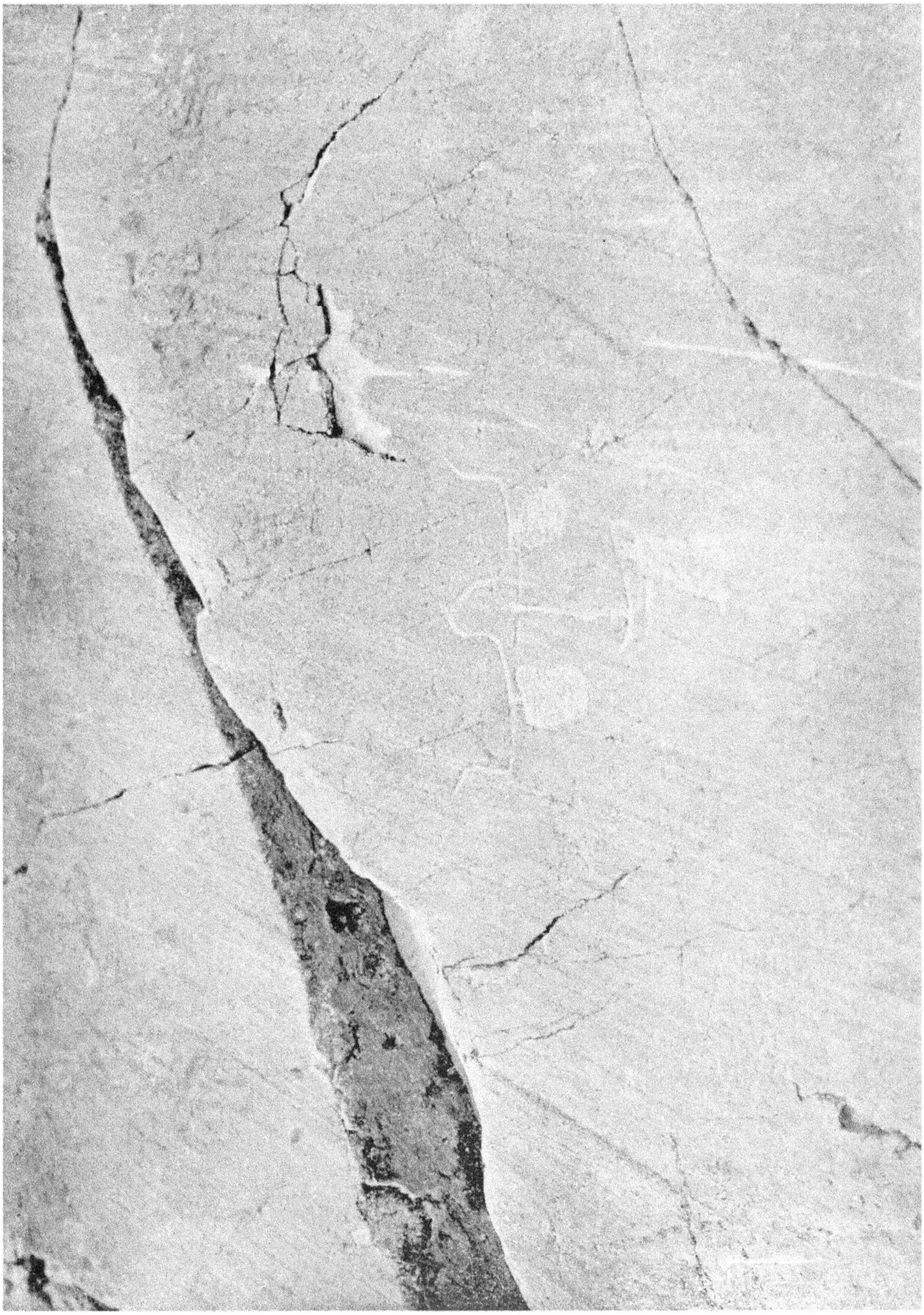

Figure of plough with oxen and three men in Val Fontanalba.

PLATE V.

1. A man ploughing in Val Casterino.

2. Plough with man on Napoleon rock.

good surfaces. In other parts they are scattered about, here one, there another, or a few on the same rock. Occasionally one lights upon a single figure in some most out of the way spot, some hidden corner, far away from others. When M. Rivière said that all the figures without exception had the same aspect, the same colour, and the same texture, so that on the second day of his sojourn he could say with certainty and at first sight whether such and such a rock was engraved or not, he was wrong, for quite near to the rocks where he worked are others of entirely different aspect with engravings. But this we have only discovered after many years, and even in our last summers we have found figures on rocks where we were quite sure there were none and so had never looked, and also on others where we had looked, but not sufficiently carefully, in former years.

The figures have nearly all been entirely cut by repeated blows of some blunt instrument, probably of quartz or other hard stone, not by metal of which no trace has been found left on them. The little round holes made by the implements vary in diameter from one to five millimetres, and are of about the same depth. Some of the figures were evidently cut by a tool or weapon held in one hand, which would account for the irregularity of the outline and the numerous outlying spots. But for many figures there is no doubt that two tools were employed, one as a chisel and the other as a hammer, and very good sharp outlines have been obtained. These are sometimes so accurate that probably the figure was traced beforehand. One of the bronze weapons would have been laid on the rock, and the contour carefully drawn. Some of these figures of weapons are the most perfectly executed, with clear sharp edges There are also plenty of engravings very badly done, either by people who had no idea at all of drawing or who could not work their rough tools. These little holes which form the figures are often so close together that the whole surface has been thoroughly cut away, but many people seem not to have had sufficient patience for such a long work, and contented themselves with only partially destroying the coloured coating. Often, and probably because the occupation was a wearisome one, a figure has not been completed. The sculptor began a plain rectangular parallelogram and had not time or patience to finish it, and this is not surprizing if he undertook a very large one. There are some figures of this kind which are a metre long and half a metre broad, and it must have taken a very long time to cut these out completely on such hard rock with indifferent tools. Sometimes figures, such as round ones, have only been cut very roughly, delineated by spots here and there, or lines have been shown by dots far apart, and give the idea of a preliminary sketch for something that was not finished. Everywhere are to be seen quantities of spots, as if done by someone who was trying his tools, though when they are crowded together or near a well-cut figure they may have some signification. There are also a few figures of which parts have been made by continuous scratching, not by blows. Some of the representations of the poles or handles of implements or weapons held by men have been so made. In some cases a natural groove or glacier scratch has been made use of and emphasized. On one rock are four figures of halberds or scythes in which the contour of the blades and the handles to which they were attached have been cut in this way (Pl. XIV-2). In no case have large pieces of the surface been flaked off, and there are never any deep holes although some of those on the hardest surfaces are the deepest of all. There are also some horned figures in which these horns have been made by cutting, not punching, and we have often found what at first sight appeared to be only small round or rectangular forms, but on looking more closely have observed that two horns had been very finely cut, but were now nearly invisible.

M. Rivière, M. Blanc, and others have said that the figures may be classed under three categories:

1. Animals.

2. Weapons, instruments etc.

3. Figures to which it is difficult to assign a meaning, but which have a certain family likeness to each other, and are of a more or less geometrical character.

When first I went to the Meraviglie, I remember thinking that the figures all represented heads of stags, weapons and nets. We now class them in eight categories:

1. Horned figures.
2. Ploughs.
3. Weapons and tools.
4. Men.
5. Huts and properties.
6. Skins.
7. Geometrical forms.
8. Miscellaneous indeterminable figures.

1. and *2. Horned figures and ploughs.*

Simple figures of an animal's head or body with two horns are by far the most abundant, and form nearly one half of the entire number. In Val Fontanalba there are about 3000; at the Meraviglie about 2000-2100. The very few figures at the head of the Valmasca valley are all horns and half of those near Col Sabbione. Only in Val Valauretta — and it is a very remarkable fact — there is not a single figure of the kind. We do not count among the numbers just given those horned figures which are joined to other ones, such as those which represent oxen with a plough, or which are arranged in some symmetrical fashion such as facing one another, or inside one another etc., but only what seem to be detached figures with two horns. These are nearly always drawn with the horns upright. Occasionally on flat surfaces the sculptors seem to have worked from different sides of the rock so that some of the horns appear to be upside down, but on inclined rocks where the sculptors must have stood at the base, horns are very rarely designedly so drawn. Sometimes they are drawn sideways, but as a rule they are all in the same direction.

These horns have been variously determined to represent those of a number of animals; the aurochs or wild European ox now extinct; the ox, stag, hind, elk, goat, ram, moufflon, sheep, chamois, ibex and perhaps others. Some writers have only seen the representation of a head or skull with the horns. M. Rivière says that there are no figures of the animals' bodies. Some have said that ears are never represented, others that they are occasionally, and that one figure is that of a hind, the horns being intended to be its ears. We ourselves think that perhaps some of the above mentioned animals may have been intended to be drawn, but we are not certain. The reason of our doubt is that we have discovered so many figures of animals evidently yoked to a plough, or yoked together though not attached to it, and which have horns of strange shapes unlike those of oxen. That there are figures of ploughs is quite certain, though no visitors before ourselves had recognized this. The horned beasts yoked to the plough must be oxen. If so the yoked beasts with strange kinds of horns must also be oxen and therefore the other figures with variously shaped horns but not yoked may possibly also be so, or at least, if not representations of oxen, be symbols of them. In the Meraviglie region we know of 36 figures of ploughs with one pair of oxen, but without any accompanying human figure. (Pl. III. 16-18.) In Fontanalba there are 81 ploughs with two beasts and with one or more human figures (Pl. III. 1-11). Two of these have three figures of men with them (Pl. III. 10-11 and Pl. IV). In some cases the two men seem to be helping to hold the handle of the plough; in others the men are standing in front of the oxen, and there is one engraving in which four oxen are yoked accompanied by a man (Pl. III.-12). There are also eleven more figures of ploughs with beasts, with which the figure of a man has probably been cut, though we cannot be sure as the rocks are so worn and broken, and there are besides 61 figures of ploughs with beasts but without any human figure (Pl. III. 13-15). In all there are 153 figures of ploughs in the Fontanalba region and the horns of the oxen vary very greatly in shape. The people who drew these could not have had cattle of many distinct races, or cattle with horns of forms quite unknown now, and it is therefore clear that the sculptors did not mean to copy from nature.

It is worthy of note that these horned figures with plough in the Meraviglie district are mostly squares with two horns (Pl. III. 16) which seem only to represent animals' heads, but in five of them there is a vertical line in addition, like a tail (Plate VI.-1) and two have also two horizontal lines on either side which may represent legs (Pl. III.-18). In the Fontanalba region the oxen in 59 figures of ploughs have tails, and in 6 have legs and tail.

Now this method of drawing a plough is an original one, and seems to be the invention of our Maritime Alps sculptors. The figure is drawn as if seen from above, looking down on the backs of the oxen, and when one day a man was ploughing in Val Casterino at the foot of a series of cultivated terraces on the hillside above, I mounted to photograph him, and the result was very much like the rock figures (Pl. V. 1). There was also an assistant gathering weeds or spreading manure just in front of the oxen, making the resemblance to some of the rock figures still more striking. This suggests to us that perhaps the prehistoric people may have cultivated terraces in the mountains, and were accustomed to look on ploughing operations from above, and so drew on the rocks what they saw. The figures of ploughs with oxen as cut on rocks in Sweden and Ireland, or painted by Egyptians and others are in profile, and the drawings done by our Fontanalba and Meraviglie people seem to be unique. Herr Stiegelmann whom we conducted to Val Fontanalba and to whom we pointed out many of the best figured rocks, says in *La Revue Préhistorique* of May 1911, that he only saw a few figures of oxen drawn in profile, and gives a copy of one on a rock which we call *The 300 Rock*. (Plate VI. 2). We are sure he is mistaken. The horned figure in question is one of the ordinary type, but adjoining or touching it is a rectangular figure, and so crowded are the figures on this particular rock that Herr Stiegelmann has taken this second figure to represent the body of an ox. We have never seen anywhere any figure of an animal drawn in profile. M. Clugnet interprets the figure which he copied on a rock near the lower Lago delle Meraviglie to be a dog in profile, but we do not agree, and believe it to be a badly executed horned figure. It is clear that some of those figures of oxen of which we have spoken represent the body, not the head of the beasts, and probably all those which have a tail do so.

Besides these complete figures of ploughs there are in the Meraviglie region 28 figures of two horned things united by a horizontal line, like yoked oxen (Pl. III. 27-29) and in Fontanalba there are 74 (Pl. III. 22-24) some of them having also a vertical line as if to indicate the pole of a plough, but without ploughshare

(Pl. III. 27). The horned figures in some of these are still less like oxen. Some are like rams' horns, some like two-pronged forks. Are these representations of oxen, or at least symbols of them? We think they are. In Fontanalba there are five figures of four horned things apparently yoked two and two (Pl. III. 25), and one of six in three pairs, and there are also eight figures where the beasts appear to be attached to what looks like a harrow, formed by two vertical or diverging lines united by several crossbars (Pl. III. 19-21 and Pl. VI. 2). One of these has not improbably the figure of a man also, but the rock is so worn that we cannot be sure.

We will now consider the horned figures, unattached to anything There are a few in both regions which certainly have branching horns, and may therefore represent some kind of deer (Pl. VII. 1-6); a few with waving or curved horizontal horns recalling those of rams; a few upright and curved ones suggesting goats, ibex or chamois (Pl. VII. 12-18); a fair number with zigzag horns like those of certain species of antelopes (Pl. VII. 19-25); and an immense number which are very like various forms of short-horned or long-horned cattle (Pl. VII. 26-33).

In many figures the lower part, the head or body, is no thicker than the horns, so that a fork rather than an animal seems to be represented (Pl. VII. 34-36), and this is like one of the letters of the Phœnician alphabet, but as these are often yoked together, and still more because sometimes there is also the figure of a ploughshare with them (Pl. III. 17), they also may represent animals. M. Rivière, who had not seen any ploughs remarks very appositely that one only arrives at the conclusion that come of these horned figures do represent animals, by following the gradual transformations between the extreme forms. When these apparent forks have a very long handle, it is certainly difficult to imagine that they can be meant for animals. They seem to be agricultural implements, such as forks now used for tossing the hay or loosening the soil (Pl. VII. 45-46). If on the other hand the bodies are greatly enlarged in size and the horns reduced, we arrive at figures which, as we shall mention later, seem to represent animals' skins.

The short concave horns also become transformed by degrees, and become more and more semicircular till they ultimately touch

PLATE VI.

1. Plough in the Arpeto region.

2. Oxen with harrow in Val Fontanalba.

and make a hoop or circle (Pl. VII. 47-51). A few have a loop attached to them (Pl. II. 52) and many more a crossbar uniting them (Pl. VIII. 1-5). Sometimes there are double parallel horns, though some of these may be two horned figures touching (Pl. VIII. 6-11). Some of the figures with four horns might represent the young antlers of deer, or two short horns and upright ears. There are also three-horned figures of various shapes (Pl. VIII. 12-17). Prof. Issel says that two pairs of horns may be pictures of monstrosities, which are not unfrequently observed, and to which the sculptors may have attributed special importance for some ritual or superstitious reason.

Many figures have a narrow kind of neck connecting the horns with the body, or it may be a thick one, more or less square or triangular (Pl. VIII. 18-19), in which case both an animal's head and body are fairly represented, and there is one type in which all the angles are right angles, and the whole figure is much more the symbol of an ox than a natural drawing of one (Pl. VIII. 38). It is astonishing how symmetrical and well cut are some of these.

The main part of the figure, whether we consider it to represent a head or a body is of many shapes, square, oval, circular, triangular etc. (Pl. VIII. 20-25). Sometimes the two sides of a triangle meet in a point below in a more natural way, but sometimes the apex is above touching the horns. Some are so long and pointed that they are just like the figures of the knives and daggers (Pl. VIII. 26), and one of the two largest horned figures, above the right bank of the Vallone delie Meraviglie, has a knife-like head only 18c. long, but two horns which are 280c. apart. (Pl. XLII. 35). This figure measures 269c. × 273c. The largest horned figure known to us on the great red Santa Maria rock in Val Fontanalba measures 316c. × 99c. and the smallest, most beautifully cut out by an immense number of blows of a very finely pointed implement measures only 1 $\frac{1}{2}$ c. × 1c. This is on the slopes of Monte Bego.

There are also sometimes large prominences between the horns, either very pronounced conical ones, or rounded humps like the tufted hair of some wild cattle or bisons (Pl. VIII. 27-31).

Some figures certainly well represent only a head with two short protruding lines below the horns to figure the ears (Pl. VIII.

44

32-36). Very rarely what we suppose to mean eyes are shown by two large spots just above the head or underneath the horns (Pl. VIII. 50-51). If the sculptors wished to represent eyes, this is the only way in which they could have done so, if all the space between the outline was cut out. We know that in many figures of weapons the rivets are shown in this manner, being drawn outside the blades. We do not know what explanation to give when one single spot has been cut above the head between the horns, and there are several of such figures (Pl. IX. 4-5). A few other figures are still more puzzling, in which a number of spots have been drawn inside or around the horns (Pl. IX. 3). Sometimes those inside take the form of small rectangular figures in regular rows (Pl. IX. 1-2). We suppose these to have had some special, perhaps a numerical meaning.

When the bodies have three projections on either side we consider that ears and legs were intended (Pl. VIII. 37, 46), even though in many cases the upper ones are as long as the lower. When there are two we think the ears have been omitted and only the legs shown (Pl. VIII. 38-45). A fifth vertical one represents a tail. These conclusions are based upon the fact that some of the figures of oxen with ploughs have these appendages. In all the Meraviglie region we only know of nine figures with tail and only one is in the region where M. Rivière worked, so that he naturally thought that no figures had a drawing of an animal's body; but in Fontanalba there are between 700-800 horned figures with tails. These are of very different lengths, often much longer than the bodies, and many of them have very conspicuous square or round knobs at their extremities, of greatly exaggerated size (Pl. VIII. 47-49), but if the flies in old times were as troublesome as they are now, the lashing of the oxen's tails continually in motion to drive away their tormentors, may have impressed some of their more tender-hearted masters, and so induced them to make a feature of this very useful appendage. If our interpretation of these ears, legs, and tails be wrong, at any rate it is convenient when speaking of the horned things to call them by these names.

Horned figures are not uncommonly drawn in groups of two or three, evidently cut in this position intentionally with a purpose

PLATE VII.

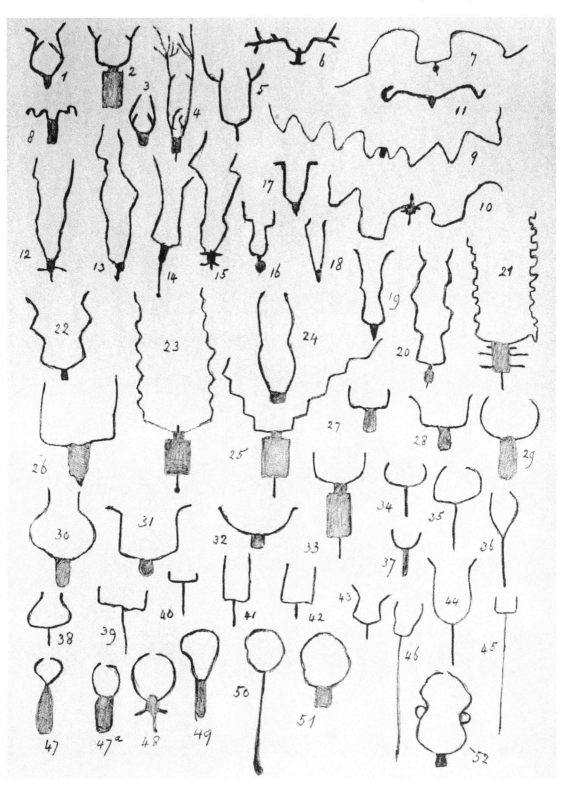

Various types of horned figures.

PLATE VIII.

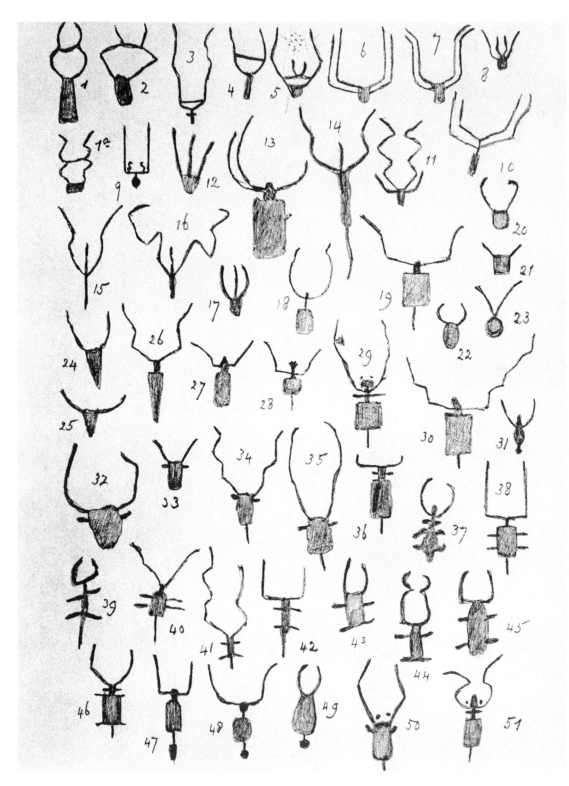

Various types of horned figures *(continued)*.

PLATE IX.

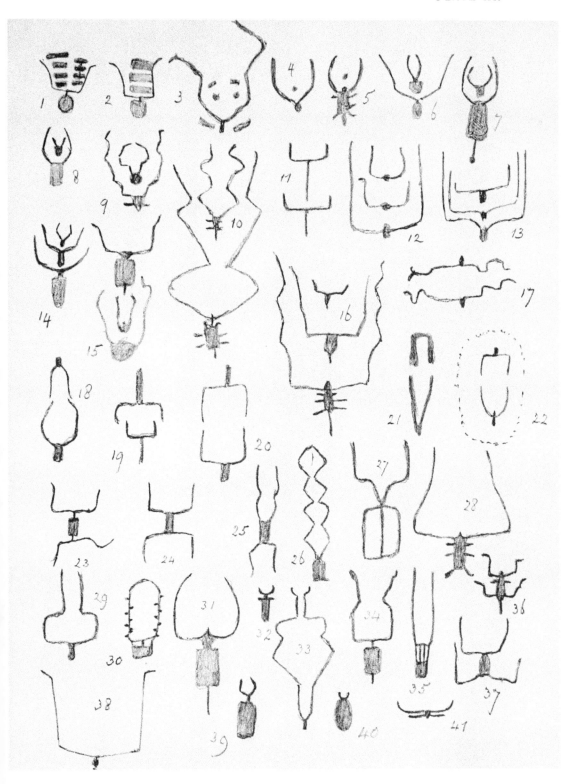

Various types of horned figures *(continued)*.

(Pl. IX. 6-16). At the Meraviglie there are twelve pairs of horns with the horns facing one another (Pl. IX. 17-21), and one pair is enclosed in a kind of oblong frame of spots, as if to point out that there was a special meaning in the arrangement (Pl. IX. 22). In Fontanalba there are three of these. The horned figures in these drawings are generally but not always of the same shape, but are always well and symmetrically arranged. What can be the meaning of these figures? Can they represent a male and female gazing at each other, or are they at all analogous to the figures from other countries of animals in profile, in what is called the heraldic position, and which are thought by some to be an attempt to represent one animal seen from both sides? In Fontanalba two horned figures are often drawn one inside the other, apparently on purpose (Pl. IX. 6-10). There are 19 of these, and there are also nine groups with three figures of horns of different sizes so arranged (Pl. IX. 12-16). There are also figures with the bodies attached to form a single body and horns facing in opposite directions, though some of these may possibly be rough drawings of a man. (Pl. IX. 23-25). In no instance, as far as we know are there any pairs of such horned figures which are not thus united.

Though there are many curious forms of horns in the Meraviglie region, the greater number of these take the forms of little forks with rectangular horns. There is a greater variety of shapes in Fontanalba, where are long spreading or upright zigzag ones, and others which have no sort of resemblance to the horns of any implements with which we are acquainted, and can only be called horned figures (Pl. IX. 26-41). We shall call attention to some of these when we speak in detail of the rocks in the various regions. In the very reduced figures of our plates the great variety of the curves and shapes of the horns cannot be thoroughly appreciated.

Besides these figures of horns by themselves, they are often combined with others. Some are cut across the handle of an implement, or fixed to the point of a blade, or placed inside or touching squares and circles, and some are joined in a row. One figure with a cross on the head has been published by M. Rivière and M. Clugnet, but we feel sure this ornament is of very much later date, and was probably added only a few centuries ago.

There are also some figures like the letters U and V. Perhaps these were finished figures, but perhaps the beginning of a horned one, for besides those uncompleted rectangular figures of which we have spoken, there are others such as a weapon without the point of the blade, or only a small part of one of the two horns, or only a part of the head. In fact there are a good many figures which do not seem to have been completed.

In order to enable our readers to see at a glance the comparative numbers of the chief varieties of these horned figures, we give the following table from the drawings we have made, but of course the numbers are open to correction.

		Meraviglie	Fontanalba
Horned figures with	ears only	7	18
»	ears and legs	1	1
»	ears and tail	—	34
»	ears, legs and tail	—	15
»	legs only	2	11
»	legs and tail	6	67
»	tail only	3	658
»	eyes	2	4

To sum up, we think that all these horned figures may be the symbols of oxen, our reason being that those which are yoked to what evidently seems a plough are of many shapes, including those not in the least like oxen. If it were not for the ploughs we could not say that any of them were really symbols of animals, for why should our sculptors have drawn them in such a strange way, instead of trying to represent them, however badly, in profile, as so many other people have done in various parts of the world? And why should so many of these oxen be represented by a more or less square head with two horns, for they are not really very much like live cattle whose ears are so very conspicuous. It is quite possible that none of the figures were really intended to represent oxen, and that the chief point of them was the pair of horns which had a special meaning; but of this we shall speak again.

PLATE X.

Horned figures in Val Fontanalba.

47

3. Weapons and tools.

We are not sufficiently acquainted with the various forms of
weapons and implements to assign names to many of those represented on the rocks. It is also difficult to say if some of them
portray those of stone or of bronze. M. Clugnet remarks that the
massive form of those he noticed, their broad blades and thick
handles, serve to show that they were made of stone, for if they
had been of metal they would have been of a slighter and more
slender shape. He also says that probably the people used these
stone instruments to cut the figures. On the other hand M. Rivière
observes that with the exception of certain figures which seem to
be intended for arrow heads and might be of stone, they all appear
to indicate weapons of bronze, and especially the triangular swords
with small narrow handles. He says that the small dimensions of
these handles seem to show that the men who used them had
small hands, and for this reason remind us of the people of India.
As for the small dimensions of the handles, that is not true with
regard to many of them, for one figure of a spear head at the
Meraviglie is 80 c. long, and has a handle too broad for anyone
to grasp. Neither of these gentlemen had seen those figures which
according to Sir Arthur Evans and others very well represent a
well known form of halberd, characteristic of the early Bronze Age
Prof. Issel does not consider these to represent halberds, but
short bronze scythes, perhaps used in religious ceremonies and
therefore ritual scythes, and which are somewhat like those found
in various parts of Sardinia, Western France and Spain. The rock
figures of the blade: with handles and rivets seem to be of three
forms; one in which the two edges of the blade are somewhat
convex, as in the figure called a halberd (Pl. XIII. 26 and XIV. 1)
one in which the upper edge is at right angles to the handle and
the lower edge straight; the third in which the blade has straight
edges of equal length. (Pl. XIV. 2). But hardly any figures of a
blade attached to its handle by rivets are drawn of the probably
natural size, and in the small figures it does not seem possible to
say for certain what kind of weapon or implement was intended
to be represented. None of these, however, appear to us to be at

all like any form of scythe or sickle which we have seen in museums.

In the Meraviglie region one cannot but be struck by the great number of weapons and implements figured. (Pl. XI., XII.). There are certainly 600, and many more if the numerous triangular figures represent blades of some kind. One rock alone near the lower lake has 12 weapons cut upon the south side and 89 on the north. There are 127 figures which represent blades fastened to handles of various lengths from 10c. to the longest of all 260c. Others have shafts of 21, 32, 68, 80, 103, 108, 121 centimetres and of intermediate lengths. Of these 11 have spots cut to indicate the rivets by which the blades were fastened (Pl. XI. 48, XII. 30, 41). A few have the blade only drawn in outline, or with horizontal lines as if to denote some ornamental grooves or ridges on them (Pl. XI. 40, 48, 49 XII. 12, 41). All these must surely represent bronze weapons or implements. Some of the figures may not improbably represent stone celts or rough tools of stone with obtuse or flat points to serve as mallets or hammers. Some figures are much like razors or scrapers. One has the form of an axe (Pl. XII. 50); a few seem to be arrow heads and sickles (Pl. XI. 35, 63, XII. 52, 60), and there are two, of which M. Rivière and M. Clugnet have given drawings, much like wooden clubs (Pl. XII. 20). There are also about eight figures to which we do not like to give a name; the blades seem to be too straight for sickles of any kind, and the handles too short in proportion to the blades to mean axes or hammers. But the greater number of the engravings represent various forms of lance or spear heads, and knives or daggers. Of these latter 40 are cut with handles separated from the blades, as if to indicate the different material, wood, bone, or horn, of the former. (Pl. XII. 14, 15, 25, 28, 40, 51). One has three spots between the blade and the handle, evidently meaning three rivets (Pl. XI. 66) and two figures have at the bottom of the detached handle, or perhaps sheath, a kind of fringe, one of eight, the other of five strands (Pl. XI. 1, 2). In about 15 the projecting hilt at the base of the blade is figured (Pl. XI. 9, 10, 65, XII. 66), and in one case at least the breadth of it seems greatly exaggerated, but it may be supposed that not all the people who occupied themselves in

PLATE XI.

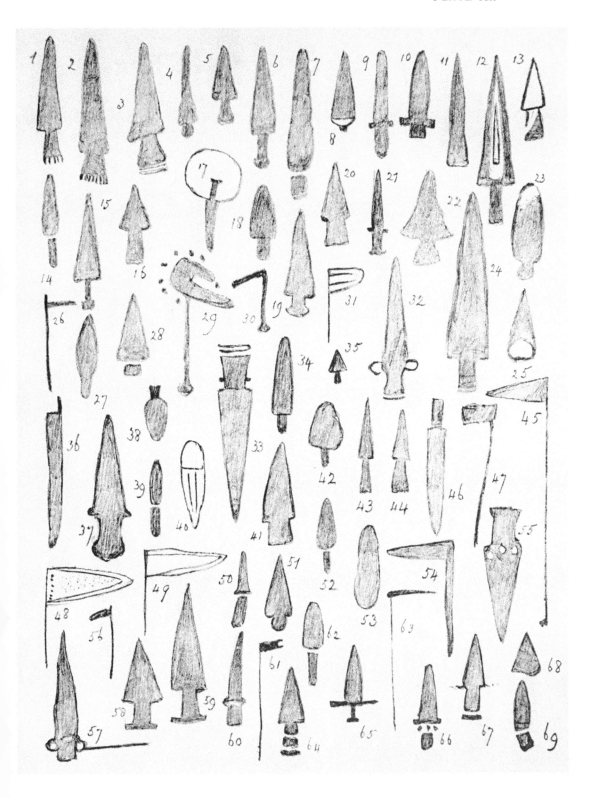

Weapons and implements in the Meraviglie region.

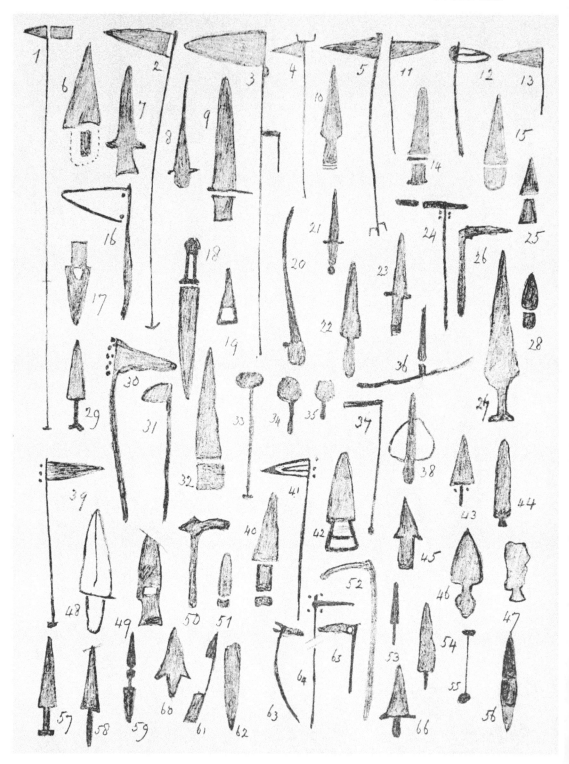

PLATE XII.

Weapons and implements in the Meraviglie region *(continued)*.

cutting figures on the rocks were good draughtsmen, and could copy accurately what they wished. The forms of weapons are, however, much more easily drawn than those of animals, and, as we have intimated, no engravings any where are so good and striking at first sight as those of the weapons, and it is not possible to mistake the meaning of them. There are three daggers with a long loop, apparently to indicate a leather strap by which it was attached to the wearer's girdle (Pl. XI. 17, XII. 38). Two of the lance heads have thongs at the base of the blade, to be used for fastit to the shaft (Pl. XI. 32). Some 13 of the daggers or spears show holes in the blades, perhaps indicating rivets, perhaps ornaments in the metal work (Pl. XI. 55, XII. 17, 49), and 3 have an ornamented handle. There are a few triangular forms of daggers, two with open handles, another with a horizontal division (Pl. XII. 19, 42). Prof. Issel has referred to a similar one figured on the Fontanalba rocks, (Pl. XIII. 62) and says that it is like an Indian dagger, except that the two openings by which the fingers can clasp it are horizontal, as in the Meraviglie figure; in the Fontanalba one they are vertical. Lastly there is a curious figure which Prof. Issel says may perhaps represent a kind of sickle (Pl. XI. 29). This we have reproduced before in two pamphlets, the second time with the addition of the seven or eight large spots surrounding it, which we had not noticed on our first visit, but which certainly form part of the engraving. There is also one small figure of a man, 22c. high, holding a weapon or implement above his head. He appears to be striking a blow, perhaps cultivating the land. (Pl. XLIII. 7).

In the Fontanalba region, though there are many more figures than at the Meraviglie, there are not half the number of weapons and implements. As far as we know there are only 236, but to make up for this inferiority, there are 36 figures of men holding up, and with one exception, in a vertical direction, a weapon or implement with long pole or handle. (Pl. XIII. 69, 70, 72-74). They are all small and much alike, except that on one rock where there are four such figures close together, the poles have not been punched out but cut and three of these have knobs cut at regular intervals along them. Whether these are merely ornaments, or were meant to emphasize the groove of the pole, or had some particular meaning we cannot say. (Pl. XIII. 69 and XVI. 1). On the Fontanalba rocks are depicted the largest and best executed figures of what have been called halberds with short handle and more or less convex blade. The best of these, to which we have already referred, measures 36c. × 38c. and the three rivets are well marked. Four other figures with short and straight-edged blades and longer handles have the contour of the blades and the handles cut (Pl. XIII. 53-56 and XIV. 2). One shows only one rivet, another two, and the others three. Another halberd figure has four rivets and a spot on either side of the blade (Pl. XIII. 23). Two others have four rivets and rings at the bottom of the handles (Pl. XIII. 8). Besides these there are 32 weapon figures of much the same shape but without any indication of rivets, and two with rivets indicated outside the semicircular end of the blade. Two others are curious, as these outside spots are connected with the blade by little lines like rays (Pl. XIII. 51-52),and finally there is one with a sort of fringe or notches at the base of the blade. (Pl. XIII. 35).

Many other figures may well represent stone celts or hammers fastened to a haft (Pl. XIII. 61). Only two daggers are engraved with handle detached from the blade. There are two of triangular form, the handle of one entirely open; the other of which we have spoken already, with a vertical division (Pl. XIII. 28, 62 and Pl. XV). Two figures are probably very curved sickles, one clearly an axe (Pl. XIII. 25, 67, 2). There are six or more arrow heads (Pl. XIII. 7), and a few things like wooden clubs or stone mallets. One dagger is ornamented by lines on the blade parallel to the sides (Pl. XIII. 60), one has a very broad hilt (Pl. XIII. 63) and, lastly, there are two weapons with straps attached. (Pl. XIII. 15).

4. *Figures of Men.*

We have already spoken of the figures of men accompanying ploughs or holding up weapons or implements. Besides these there are certainly in Fontanalba 15 figures of men, mostly very small, the largest and best drawn being only 19c. × 11c. (Pl. XIII. 71, 76, 77). Six or seven of these are close together with some horned and other figures, and may perhaps form part of a group intended to

Weapons and implements in Val Fontanalba.

Figures of men and men with implements.

represent a settlement with huts, enclosures and cattle. Three other human figures close by on the same rock seem to be standing round a pair of yoked oxen with a harrow, and with them is also a figure of a man with an implement and two figures of enclosures. These two groups are more like living scenes than any others on all the rocks, but as the surface is crowded with figures, and they seem to have been cut by different hands or by different tools, we cannot say if they really form groups which were intended to form a picture. As we shall explain more fully later, the more we study these rock figures, the less are we able to believe that, except very rarely, the juxtaposition of the figures has any meaning. At the Meraviglie there is one figure which seems to be that of a man pulling a harrow or dragging a net (Pl. XXXVIII. 35) and a certain number which are not improbably meant for human figures, though they may be those of two horned ones joined together when there is no clear indication of a head. (Pl. XLII. 17, 18). There are certainly five separated and detached figures of men, besides the one already mentioned. One of these was published by M. Rivière, who says that Mr Moggridge had drawn it very incorrectly; but Mr Moggridge's figure, which was also drawn by M. Clugnet, we well know, and is much farther up the valley. The one given by M. Rivière is probably seen by everybody who goes up to the Meraviglie lake, as it is close to the path most frequented. A third is high up towards the crest of the slopes above the right bank of the Vallone. The fourth deserves special notice, as it is extremely interesting. It is in one of those hidden unlikely places where we believe that noone but ourselves is ever likely to have gone. It is near the stream on the right bank of the Vallone, a little below the lake. The rock, a loose block, lies among a quantity of others of the same kind, and can only be reached by climbing up and down among them. It is quite hidden from the opposite bank and from the track above. No sort of path passes it, and there is no sort of vegetation to attract even the omnivorous goats. Only persons intent on prying into every hole and corner of the whole region would ever have thought of going or looking there. The rock has a polished yellow surface turned towards the cliff, and on it are twelve or more figures very well cut, and we think that many of them, if not all, were cut by the same hand. There are five weapons, one with a strap, and two others with their handles facing in symmetrical fashion. There is a large sort of rectangular figure with many divisions, two or three horned ones, a small figure of a man with uplifted arms like an Orante in the Roman catacombs, one or two collections of spots, and lastly the large man which we call *The Chief of the Tribes*. (Pl. XVII.). This very strange figure reminds us of the Devil-dancers or Witch-doctors of savage tribes. The arms are stretched out horizontally, the fingers well delineated. A small V does duty for eyes and nose. The neck, shoulders and lower part of body, unless some sort of skirt is intended, are entirely punched out. The sex is clearly marked, and the legs end in feet turned inwards. But in the middle of the square outline which indicates the breast or some piece of clothing, is one of the ordinary simple horned figures, which in this central position seems to acquire some important meaning. We shall refer to this again presently.

5. 6. 7. Huts and Properties, Skins and Geometrical Figures.

We now come to the third of M. Rivière's divisions, adding to those which he calls geometrical figures, and to his indeterminable signs but which are more or less of the same type, two other classes of figures which we feel sure must represent properties of some kind and animals' skins.

We will first speak of the Fontanalba region. Here there are about 240 figures of squares, circles and other closed figures indicated by straight or curved lines. Perhaps the simple rectangular or more or less circular ones may represent enclosures for sheep or cattle. In the mountains where stones lie about everywhere it is easy to build up rapidly rough walls, and in times when wild beasts abounded and there were wolves, and probably wild men of other unfriendly tribes, such protective shelters might be much needed. The shepherds of today have told us that the small ones of which one sees the remains here and there were used in old times to shelter a ewe with its lamb, though nowadays they neither make nor use such shelters. Larger ones with a few divisions would well represent folds and pens: but when we come to consider those figures which

PLATE XIV.

1. Halberd in Val Fontanalba.

2. Somewhat similar figures.

PLATE XV.

Rock surface in Vallone della Rocca with triangular dagger.

PLATE XVI.

1. Men with implements in Val Fontanalba.

2. Similar figures.

PLATE XVII.

The 'Chief of the Tribes,' Vallone delle Meraviglie.

have a great number of divisions, we think they must have some other explanation. They might be harrows or hurdle barriers. About a dozen of these figures of enclosures have spots inside them. (Pl. XVIII. 1-13, 16-20). There are from 300 to 350 figures such as squares, right-angled parallelograms, oblongs, circles etc. entirely cut out, and some of these are of immense size; but there are also quantities of quite small ones. Many are badly cut with very irregular edges, but many, and especially the rectangular ones, are cleanly done. About 24 of these latter have a line stretching out from the narrow side, and roughly resemble a spade, or as we think, may represent a hut with path leading to it (Pl. XVIII. 21-23). All these forms are quite a feature of this valley, and especially when they are united to one or more curved or rectangular enclosures. (Pl. XVIII. 24-30). About 170 of the simplest forms of these, that is, a rectangular figure with semicircle or other sort of closed line joining it, are cut on the Fontanalba rocks, and we look upon these as signifying huts or sheds with a piece of ground enclosed by a wall. They may also very probably represent a rock with the same, for we have often seen such among the broken-down enclosures of old days. The rock serves as a shelter from wind or sun, and sometimes a space has been enclosed on both sides of it. The shepherds have often made folds of a rude kind for their sheep by utilizing several large rocks, and joining them together by walls, and have thus saved much labour and made more secure shelters. But the regularity of these figures better suggests that they represent huts. Where there are now herds of cattle there are generally several simple rudely constructed huts. In one the butter is made; in another the cheeses are stored until ripe and ready to be taken down to market; and in another the cowherds sleep. In these days the huts are sometimes built better and have a decent roof with ridgepole and planks, but three easily made walls with branches of larch trees placed across the top of them, or some sailcloth, are sufficient for a summer habitation. At some of the large Margherie an enclosure into which the cattle are driven to be milked and in which they sleep, is formed of larch poles, but on many mountain sides may be seen the remains of the old walls which once enclosed areas of considerable size.

54

One particular feature of these Fontanalba figures of enclo-- sures is that very often there are quantities of spots cut in them. In about 100 of these the spots are of the same size, mere dots made by a single blow of the tool and scattered about in a haphazard sort of way; but when there are two or more enclo- sures, or in figures of the same type but more complicated, there are spots of two kinds, small in some areas and large in others. (Pl. XVIII. 31, 40, 43-45). These large spots have been produced by repeated blows, sometimes forming large more or less round holes; but sometimes they are in regular rows and deeply cut, taking the form of short thick lines. There are more than 50 of these figures with the large spots, and the number of the spots can always be counted. When sometimes passing up Val Fontanalba in the early morning, or returning late towards evening, we have seen the white cows standing or lying down within their larch-pole enclosure, close to three rectangular sheds, we have been very much struck by the resemblance of the scene to these rock figures, and have wondered if the spots cut inside the figure might not be a representation of the sculptors' herds. Might not the large and conspicuous spots indicate the cows in one enclosure, and the immense number of small dots represent sheep and goats in the other? When the cattle go up to the higher Margheria in the valley where the pasture for sheep and goats begins, we often see them all near together, and the former when looked at across the valley, are very conspicuous. They sometimes seem to be standing in regular rows and can be pretty accurately counted, but the smaller animals scattered about in much larger numbers cannot. If the sculptors who engraved figures to represent their ploughs and oxen, and probably their sheds also, had wished to portray one of their dwelling places with their flocks and herds, they could hardly have done so in a more lifelike though symbolic manner.

Some entire rocks are covered with figures of these two kinds, with perhaps a few accompanying horned ones as well, and they seem to make a complete picture, a kind of plan of a settlement or village of huts for men and pens for beast. Two are very remarkable, and we call them *The Skin Hill Village* (Pl. XLIII. 4) and *The Monte Bego Village* (Pl. XIX. 2 and Pl. XLIV. 1) and there are many others similar but of a more complicated kind. One rock has a number of little sheds, as we will call them, all connected with one another by lines, and the whole enclosed in a circle, as if it were a village with protective wall around it, (Pl. XVIII. 41). Other rocks have numbers of large more or less rectangular figures with lines, to which we cannot give any interpretation, and one great orange surface, but very worn, has an elaborate design of figures like the Egyptian cartouches, with oblong figures inside them entirely cut out, and lines connecting the cartouches. There are no figures like these in the Meraviglie district.

There is another rectangular form common in and almost peculiar to Val Fontanalba. This seems to represent the skin of a beast. These are chiefly near Lago Verde and in the lower part of what we call *Skin Hill*, on account of the number of such figures there, and occur either in the simplest form, or in combination with other sorts of figures. There are about 90 of these. Some of them have projections at two corners, like the skins of two legs; some at all four, and some have a tail as well. (Pl. XX. 1-4, 8-10). Others have loops, sometimes on two sides (Pl. XX. 11-13). One has on both sides a number of horizontal lines and looks like a gigantic centipede (Pl. XX. 14) and some have large spots here and there round them (Pl. XX. 5, 6). All these suggest skins laid out to dry, and held down by ropes or fastened to large stones, but we do not venture to suggest interpretations of many of the numerous varieties, of which a skin seems to be the chief part of the design (Pl. XX. 15-22). Here we may mention that there are four figures of spirals and two of concentric circles (Pl. XVIII. 14, 15). To one other, which may be classed among the geometrical figures, we have already alluded. On four narrow, smooth, parallel surfaces of a yellow rock, and at different elevations, are four long scalariform figures, that is, long parallelograms with horizontal bars. One is divided into 14, another into 15, and a third into 20 compartments. The fourth figure is divided into three parts by two vertical lines, and the parts contain 18, 18 and 10 partitions. In most of these partitions are spots. Some have one, some 2, 3, 4, or more, up to 8, and a few an indefinite number. The other three figures have nothing cut in the partitions. These figures must surely be a record of the enumeration of cattle or other possessions, or at least be some kind of account and have a numerical signification. (Pl. XXI. 1, 2).

In the Meraviglie region the simple enclosed figures such as squares, circles, and combinations of them, abound. There are about 250 of them. There are also seven figures of concentric circles. Of the rectangular figures with an enclosure there seem to be only 15, and only one has dots inside. But there are a very great number of most complicated figures, some of great size, and many of them most irregular and unsymmetrical. These form one of the most conspicuous features of the Vallone delle Meraviglie and the slopes above both banks of it. We know of nearly 100. It was suggested by M. Rivière, and his idea accepted by others, that some at least of these may represent nets, or else barriers into which game might be driven at the narrow part of a defile. The more regular forms might mean nets of some material for carrying down hay or straw. We can only say that many of them do not seem to represent anything with which we are acquainted, and we have no idea what they represent. The contours are of very varied shapes, and the spaces within divided up in all sorts of ways, and look just like a dissected map or a jig-saw puzzle. (Pl. XXII., XXIII., XXIV).

8. Miscellaneous indeterminable figures.

We have now spoken of the chief types of figures in the two principal regions. Those which cannot well be placed in any of those classes we shall speak of when describing those regions more minutely. (See figures of Plates XXV., XXX., XXXII., XXXIV., XXXVII., XXXVIII., XLI., XLII). We have seen that the same kinds of people and of the same period cut the figures, and that though on both sides of the dividing crest of Monte Bego the same forms of horns and weapons were engraved, and the same way of depicting a plough was adopted, there are very noticeable differences. In Fontanalba figures of men with ploughs and weapons, forms of the skin type, and of huts with enclosures are conspicuous. At the Meraviglie are a greater variety of weapons and large labyrinthine and quasi-geometrical figures, while in the intermediate valley of

PLATE XVIII.

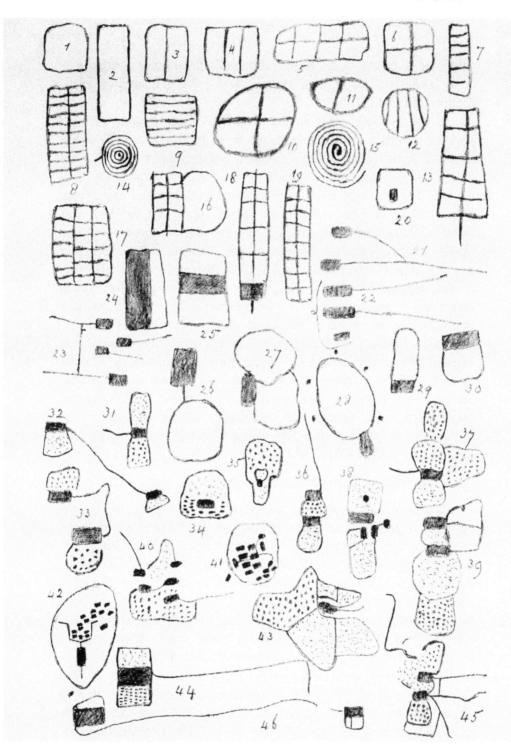

Geometrical figures, huts with enclosures etc. Val Fontanalba.

Valauretta there are only geometrical ones akin to those in Fontanalba, and not one single weapon or pair of horns. We can believe
that there were different tribes settled in different places not far
away, and that some were more engaged in agriculture and the
rearing of flocks and herds, and others more occupied with hunting
wild animals, and that their methods of following a common practice somewhat changed in many years, just as dialects rapidly do
in valleys separated by lofty mountains; but it is very difficult to
understand why the people who went into Val Valauretta showed
so little variety of work, and did not imitate more closely that of
their near neighbours on either side of them.

CHAPTER V.

Modern Inscriptions.

The modern writings and drawings on the rocks have a certain amount of interest for various reasons. One is that they help to reassure us of the great age of the prehistoric ones, because they look so white and new in comparison with them. Another is that they seem to show that the figures began to be known and attract attention about four centuries ago, at least in the Meraviglie region. We think that people must have gone up on purpose to see them, as nearly all the 16th and 17th century inscriptions are near together on beautiful surfaces close to the best prehistoric ones. The date 1727, very clearly cut, is the earliest we have seen in Val Fontanalba. In 1776 some one named *Antonio Dolsa* scratched his name twice, once adding a not badly drawn figure of a beast with the words *"I have done this lion."* We here desire to commemorate this artist unknown to fame. On a rock near Lago Verde is the date 1835 with spirited picture of a horse, and at the head of the valley a more elaborate one of Napoleon III on horseback with dogs, and women offering flowers to the soldiers. This bears the inscriptions *" Ti Napoleon torna i la tua Francia e lassa il Piemonte. Giuseppe Lanterio di Tenda, 1849."* Under this is written *"Li 30 Agosto, 1849, anno de la Repubblica e de la libertà."* This seems to show that the writer was a disciple of Mazzini, and disapproved of the suppression of the Roman Republic. Now this picture, which is the chef d'œuvre in our modern mountain picture gallery, is very well known, and apparently so also are the other similar ones. The shepherds have spoken about them to each other. An alpine guide whom I questioned about the prehistoric engravings, wanting to know what he thought about them, answered that he had not himself seen any in Val Fontanalba, but he knew that there were some of horses and dogs. We suspect

PLATE XIX.

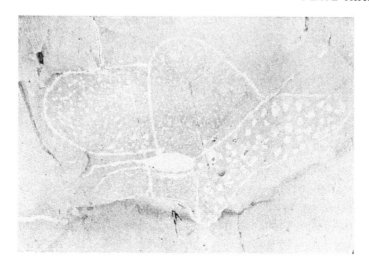

1. Napoleon rock, Val Fontanalba

2. Part of the 'Monte Bego Village.'

that all the shepherds who go up there find out the celebrated Napoleon rock. One certainly, a friend of ours, knows it only too well, for he has cut his name in large letters right across some of the best prehistoric figures with which the rock is covered. He has done the same in many other places, but we have remonstrated with him, and believe he now understands the value of the old work, and will for the future respect it. As a rule the prehistoric figures have not been seen by the shepherds, and in any case do not interest them, but those who can read and write are pleased to find the names of other shepherds whom they know, if not personally, at least by name, and sometimes themselves record that they passed by with a certain number of sheep on a certain day, or bewail the sad fact that they have no pipe or tobacco. These men do not imitate the old engravings, and very rarely do any of them deface the rocks. Would that we could say the same of some of the more educated visitors!

In the Meraviglie region the modern cuttings are much more interesting. On the way up the Vallone the path on the right bank passes a high polished vertical rock wall. Only the last time we were there did we notice that there are two roughly cut prehistoric figures of weapons on it close to the ground, but it is covered with countless names and initials. It seems to serve the same purpose as a bottle for cards on a mountain summit, and is really useful, as visitors spend their superfluous energy in inscribing their illustrious names there, and so leave the valuable figured rocks higher up in peace. Among the names and inscriptions in various languages on this wall is one cut in large letters as befits so well known a man, BENSA, 1829. He was a notorious highwayman who is said to have been the terror of Tenda and all the neighbouring country about the year 1825. He has also left his name deeply incised on the top of Monte Bego. He was at last caught in France and executed. The greater number of modern marks are above the right bank of the Vallone, and on some rocks are more numerous than the ancient ones. The earliest ones we have seen are *1513 et dies 3; 1520; 1526 dies...* with something we cannot decipher, and *1546* with the inexplicable words 'de fam fmar.' The date 1593 is on a rock near the upper lake, and we have heard of another of the 16th century but have not seen it. Dates of the next century are more abundant, the century in which the priest Laurenti spoke and Gioffredo wrote about the place. We have noticed *B. G. 1607; Gio. Batt. Saorgino* with apparently the same date; also *Cesare Pachiaudi di Saorgio.* Families of these names still live in Saorgio, and the former also at Fontan, which is a kilometre farther north, and was till forty years ago a hamlet of Saorgio. Besides these are *Bartholomeo Guido di Tenda; Antonio Bosio di Tenda 1619,* and *Claudio Salvagno di Tenda 1619.* There is no family of the latter name now living there, and Tenda people told us that they had never heard of such a family, but Dr Mader, through the kindness of Signor Degiovanni, has lately discovered a register in the parish archives dated 29th. July, 1631, to this effect; " A daughter of Signor Claudio Salvagno and of his wife Caterina, who was born on the 25th instant, has been baptized by me Giovanni Arnolfo the parish priest. Her name has been called Magdalena." Then follow the names of her godfather and godmother. It seems not unlikely that this is the person, probably of good family, who had cut his name twelve years before in letters which today look only a little less new than those of M. Rivière in 1887. The ciphers are of a form no longer used. Near this is the best of all the modern works, a very large and well executed coat of arms. The shield, surmounted by a helmet, bears several conventional fleurs-de-lys and other charges, and above is a long-armed cross. Underneath is the well known motto *' Malo mori quam fœdari '* (better death than dishonour) with *VV. Humberto del Agarena, Viennese, 1629.* We have tried to find out if there was a knight of Malta of that name, for the form of the cross seems to indicate that he was one, but have not succeeded. On the same rock are cut in Greek letters LAGATHROOS which seem to have no meaning, and also some Hebrew ones Jan Irock. Another person has cut the sacred monogram I. H. S. surmounted by a cross, and followed by a heart transfixed by three arrows, with *1659 li 25 Luglio,* and not far off the same person apparently in the following year made a very elaborate decoration with the words *1660 li 8 Agosto. Amore fecit. A. C. Saorgio,* with I. H. S. and the cross, all enclosed in a sort of ornamental frame. Besides

PLATE XX.

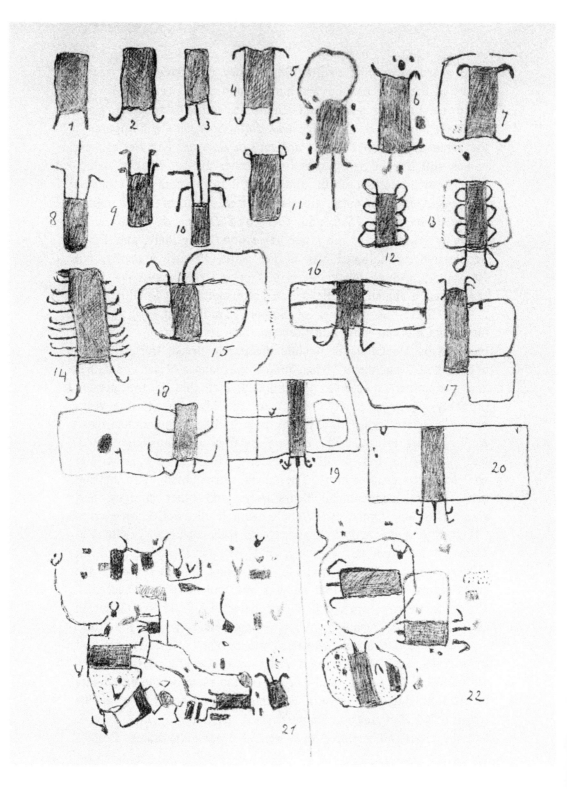

Skins and figures of skin type. Val Fontanalba.

these are *G. B. T. 1657; 1668 G. R.* and *Claudio Cabagno 1684*, and others. Of the next century we find *Giovanni Cassio 1717; 1718, 13 Agosto* without name, and the dates 1726, 1728 with a cross, *13 Agosto B. G.* with two crosses etc. On the other side of the valley near the lake is a mere scratch, invisible most of the day but extraordinarily clear in the early morning light, *Gian Battista Guidi, 1 Agosto 1766,* and underneath *1770 reduce,* from which we gather that the same person returned four years later. After these there do not seem to be any names or dates till about 30 or 40 years ago, since which time much has been scratched. These later ones have probably been made by shepherds who had frequented the communal schools, but the early ones must have been done by educated people, sportsmen, alpinists or visitors to the Meraviglie, for it is highly unlikely that shepherds were able to write in those days. We once spoke to two shepherds in this region. They told us they had heard there were writings on the rocks, but they could not read. We were standing on a rock covered with prehistoric figures, and asked if they saw anything cut there. They looked and said no, and were much astonished when we pointed out the very numerous figures of horns and weapons. The same thing occurred in Fontanalba, and long after we had left we saw the man walking about the large surface evidently interested in his discoveries. It would seem that the supposed tradition of Hannibal's soldiers having left their records on the rocks is not very widely known now, and what there is to be seen not much more. We have only met one man who said he knew who had done the engravings, for his grandmother had told him that they had been made by the French soldiers at the end of the 18th century. Directly above the mines we have seen the words *RAULA TIACA RETRINO 1008.* Perhaps the date may be intended for 1608 and the words for Realdo Triora Petrino, Realdo being a village in the commune of Triora from which Pietro may have come. Shepherds often cross over from there, and this rock was pointed out by one, and was known to him as a very smooth one on which they were accustomed to sharpen their knives. Perhaps the frequent recurrence of sacred symbols, the cross and I. H. S. show that a few centuries ago the people thought that the neighbourhood of Cima del Diavolo and Val d' Inferno was a dangerous one, and they cut those signs which they believed to have the power of warding off evil spirits. An old peasant friend in the country has told us that when he was a boy the world was full of witches and goblins who plagued and maltreated people in all sorts of ways, but since then they have been excommunicated, and are now safely shut up underground.

PLATE XXI.

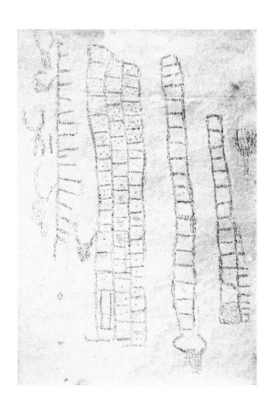

The 'Scala di Paradiso' rock in Val Fontanalba.

1. From a photograph. 2. From a rubbing.

CHAPTER VI.

The Authorship and Meaning of the Engravings.

Mr Moggridge says "I could discern no writing in the ordinary acceptation of the word. If any meaning is to be attached to these designs, they must be read as hieroglyphics. The fact that the figures are frequently repeated and in different combinations, just as our letters are to form words, may accord with the supposition that they have a meaning." M. Riviere speaks of "hieroglyphics or symbolic signs, which are repeated more or less frequently on the same or on different rocks, and in combinations sometimes the same but often different." Signor Navello thinks the inscriptions contain no symbolic language; the disorder of the figures which are not in lines; the fact that some are intercalated among others which are more ancient; the diverse dimensions of the figures which represent the same object although placed close to each other; and lastly the absence of human forms and living scenes, towers and chariots of war, absolutely exclude the idea of a symbolical language destined to preserve the memory of warlike deeds." M. Blanc says that "with the exception of an armed man erroneously considered by M. Clugnet to be perhaps a bird, no living scene is represented; there are only separate objects of different age, and cut in such disorder that it is impossible to find any sequence of ideas etc."

In consequence of these remarks. and still more because Prof. Issel has several times said that more attention should be paid not only to the separate figures, but also to the groups resulting from their juxtaposition, we have in these last years given much time to copying where possible, on very large sheets of paper, some of these groups, and often the whole surface of a rock; and we have now a large collection of these rubbings, some measuring as much as 358c. $\times$ 120c., 300c. $\times$ 100c., 240c. $\times$ 140c. etc., and a great many more on sheets of about one square metre. It is extremely difficult to make these large drawings, for however still the air may seem to be when we begin, there is always enough wind soon after to blow the paper about, and if fastened down by heavy stones we cannot copy so correctly. Also on convex surfaces, or those where the figures are upon different levels, we cannot map out the rock into equal partitions, and fit our drawings together to form the complete picture as it ought to be.

We are convinced after long study of these rocks, that there is very rarely any sign of order in the arrangements of the figures. Probably there are not a dozen rocks where there are figures in straight lines like the letters of writing. Sometimes horns are more or less in a horizontal row, and, as we have said, three of these are sometimes placed symmetrically in a vertical line. There are a few examples of different kinds of figures in a row close together but not touching one another, and others where they do touch and make as it were one complete figure. They are often joined together in many ways, where there was plenty of unoccupied space on the rock to cut them apart. A number of horns or of figures of diverse kinds often interlace each other. These may perhaps be considered to form a group having some signification. Then there are rocks where the figures, mostly horned ones and all pointing in the same direction, seem to make a completed work, and there are those, of which we have already spoken, which do unmistakeably seem to be an intentional design, such as those which we have called villages, encampments or Margherie. There is one bright yellow surface close to the right bank of the stream from the upper lake which has a large engraving measuring 350c. $\times$ 100c. and consisting of four large enclosed spaces touching one another vertically. In these are cut two ploughs and thirteen horned beasts with a few more outside. (Pl. XLIII. 1). On another rock under M. S. Maria is a group of 81 beasts and a rectangular figure with six divisions, all of which are contained within a huge rectangular line or frame.

On the rocks pretty thickly covered with figures we can sometimes pick out a certain number which seem to form a group though they may not be more isolated than an equal number on any other part of the rock; but when rocks are densely covered

PLATE XXII.

Geometrical and complicated figures. Meraviglie region.

PLATE XXIII.

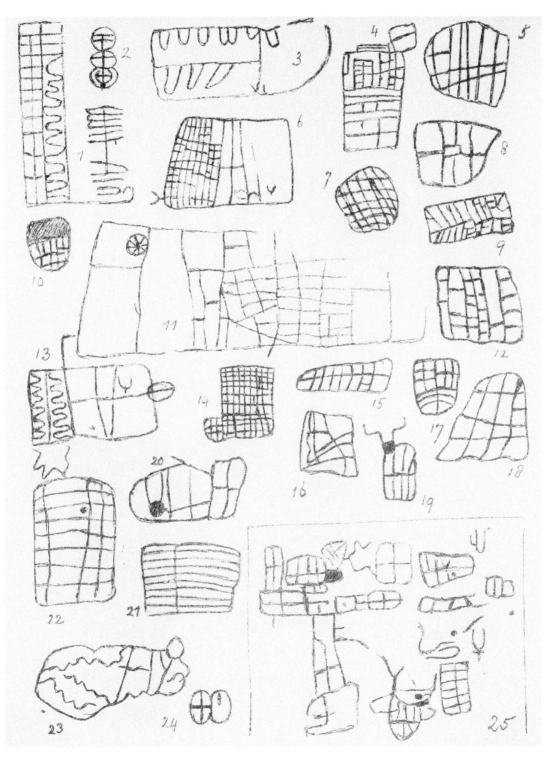

Geometrical and complicated figures Meraviglie region. *(continued).*

PLATE XXIV.

1. Figures on a rock in the 'Défilé.'

2. Figures on M. Rivière's rock.

with figures it is impossible to pick out any particular set to form a group. We think that some rocks became popular places of resort, and that the sculptors went there year after year to add something to the work of their predecessors. The sight of the figures done by others would have induced them to assist in covering the rock. In places now visited by tourists or at some sanctuary, we see a particular spot covered with names just as we see them on the walls of the Roman catacombs. What we call '*The 300 Rock*' in Val Fontanalba is so crowded with ploughs and horns and enclosures, that there is hardly any clear space left, and the northern slope of '*The Altar Rock*' at the Meraviglie, with its 84 weapons and over 220 horned figures, is even more densely covered. On this rock we have copied some 450 figures, and are not sure if we have yet finished. On this there seems to be only one set of interlacing horns which may be called a group. (Pl. XLII. 38). On the other hand there are rocks with a great many figures but scattered about in a very irregular way, and where there does not appear to be any idea of intentional juxtaposition.

One of the great difficulties in coming to any decision in many cases as to whether there are groups or not is that we cannot decide if the figures were cut at the same time or not. Sometimes it appears to us quite certain that they were not. Figures looking much newer have not only been made close to others looking older, but have actually been cut across them. I published in my *Further Explorations etc. Plate VIII. fig. 30* a drawing of a weapon with a horn across the top of the blade. In 1911 I discovered that the supposed horn was really a part of three lines of a large geometrical figure, the greater part of which was nearly obliterated and hardly visible. In this case there is no doubt that one is very much older than the other, but in some cases there may have been a meaning in one figure having been cut across another. Though there is often this great difference in the apparent ages of figures close together, they may have been done at the same time, but owing to the use of different tools, or to the greater or less strength of the blows, some of the figures have worn well and others badly. There is also often a great difference in the appearance of figures on the two slopes of a convex surface, on account of the laminated structure of the schist. One side is much weathered and the other not. Rocks close together and equally covered with figures may also present a very different appearance, as one of them may have been covered by snow every year till late into the summer, and so protected from the early and late frosts which have split the other. Over some rocks water runs almost constantly and they have lost their original colour, and the figures look much older though they really may not be so. For all these and perhaps other reasons it is not easy to say if a certain number of figures near together on the same rock were cut-to form a group which had a meaning. We are inclined to believe that where there does seem to be a group of figures, they were in many cases executed not by one person but by many, for the technic of the work is often so different, but of course such a group may have been some kind of record or contract which many people assisted in engraving. It is not difficult to distinguish the different handiwork of different sculptors.

To sum up we may say that there are:

1. Certainly small complete pictures of oxen yoked to a plough or harrow with one man or more.

2. Probably pastoral scenes such as enclosures with cattle or other animals inside.

3. Probably pictures of Margherie, or groups of sheds with enclosures for beasts, or plans of land divided in various ways and with paths etc., or, as Prof. Issel suggests, the same with ponds or drinking places.

4. Complex engravings composed of more or less similar forms joined together and making a picture the meaning of which we cannot guess.

5. Figures of common types such as horns or geometrical ones apparently purposely joined together or quite close to one another, the signification of which is equally obscure.

Only one rock, as far as we know, has some figures in a row which give the idea of a sequence of alphabetical forms. They seem to belong to another figure of geometrical type, and all of them to have been cut by the same hand. (Pl. XXIII. 1). Of these Prof. Issel says "I cannot help thinking that this is an ensign composed of several symbolical figures, and accompanied by an inscription analogous to what is seen in many coats of arms." These forms do certainly look like letters, but if the people knew of such things it is very strange that we do not find more of them in combination. But though there seems to be only this one figure which looks much like a row of letters, there are certainly plenty of engravings like well-known early alphabetical forms or symbols. One of the commonest types of horns on the Meraviglie ròcks, a fork with two parallel vertical prongs, is an archaic Phoenician character. So is a rectangle with a crossbar. Stars with six or eight rays, squares and rectangular figures divided by vertical and one or two horizontal lines are, according to Sir A. Evans, of the Mycenaean epoch in Crete. Circles, two concentric circles with spots in the middle, a three-pronged fork, and a vertical line with short horizontal arm are Cretan and Libyan figures. In the Etruscan alphabet are circles with spots, or with one or two diameters, and two-horned or three-horned figures. Some of these are found on dolmens in France, and some on rocks in the Canaries. The figures Pl. XXXVIII. 41, XLI. 29, 40, 51, XLII. 13, 14 Prof. Issel thinks may be alphabetical letters or private marks like our initials or abbreviations. He also suggests that those horizontal lines of the linear figures which we have taken to mean the ears or legs of an ox, or at least the symbol rather than the representation of one, may have a numerical meaning, such as one, two, or three oxen, or oxen of one, two or three years. He also gives very many interesting and ingenious explanations of many other figures in his *Liguria Preistorica* pp. 485-559, to which we must refer our readers.

We do not know if there are any grounds for the belief that Phœnicians discovered the mines of Tenda, and that the old galleries long since abandoned were their work. Prof. Celesia thinks that our rock figures, so near the mines, were executed by them. He says they may have been a long time in the neighbourhood searching for metals, and that whereever they went they left behind them the signs of their presence in hieroglyphics. From their headquarters at Marseille they would have passed through Antibes and

68

Turbia, and by the Col di Tenda into Piedmont. The historian Guizot says expressly that this was the Via Erculea. In answer to this we would only remark that the Phœnicians did not know the use of lead, which is the chief product of the Tenda mines, whereas other metals, silver, zinc and copper, have only been found there in very small quantities, so that they would not have made there the bronze weapons which are figured on the rocks; and did they not always leave behind them memorials of a far higher class than those of our rude figures? In the *Revue Archéologique 1908* Monsieur G. Doublet gives an account of a small bronze statue which he had received from an Italian workman, and was said to have been found by him in the mines, but other manufactured articles also said to have been found there have not been seen by competent authorities. Dr Mader thinks that some of the figures of a man with implement might represent a miner wielding his powerful hammer, but we doubt if men working in the mines would have been likely to cut figures of ploughs and oxen in such large numbers. It is more probable that tribes inhabiting those parts might have received bronze weapons from Phœnicians who landed on the coast and passed across the mountains. Romans also in later times are said to have worked the mines, but if so they have left no sign of their presence, and they had swords and other weapons of iron. There is also the tradition that Saracens, who for about fifty years in the 10th Century raided these valleys, used the mines, but as Mahometans they did not carve representations of men, and in any case they as well as the Romans may be dismissed, as the rock engravings surely date from long before they came upon the scene.

M. Rivière believes that the sculptors were of Libyan origin. He finds a great resemblance between our figures and those discovered in Morocco in the province of Sous. He says that they are made in exactly the same way by repeated blows of some blunt instrument, and that some of the figures are identical. At the same time he admits that there are no drawings of weapons on the African rocks, and only 'a sort of head analogous to one of those in the first group,' although others are very like the geometrical ones of the Meraviglie. There are not, however, many

PLATE XXV.

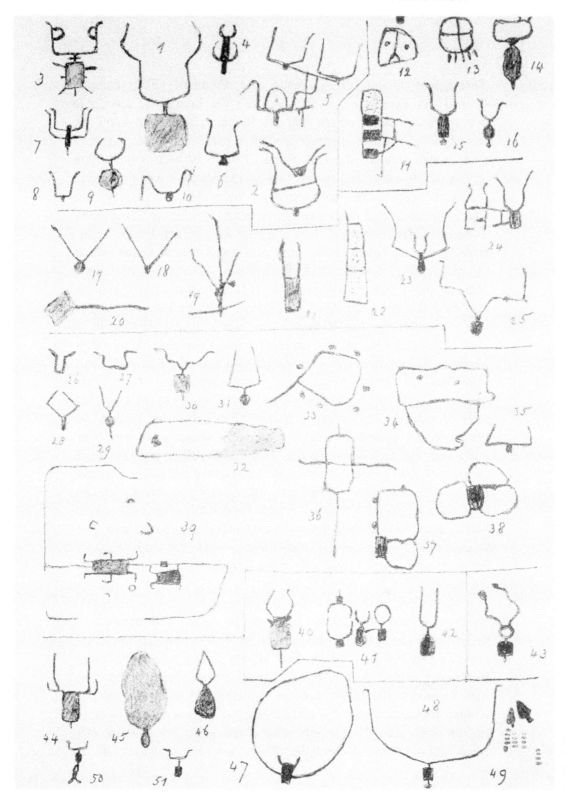

Figures in Val Fontanalba.

methods of making figures on hard rock surfaces. Either the outlines may be cut like the well-known figures on horns, or the figures may be entirely punched out, and on our very hard rocks, as on the volcanic ones in Morocco, the punching of the figures would appear to be the simplest and easiest method for people without very fine tools. Moreover as horns and weapons are by far the most numerous forms with us, the entire resemblance to the figures in Morocco does not seem very close.

D'Albertis in his *Crociera del Corsaro* gives copies of the figures cut on the rocks in the island of Hierro in the Canary group, but with one or two exceptions they do not. appear, as he himself allows, to have much, if any, resemblance to ours. There spirals and strange curves are common, but the former of these are extremely rare with us, and the latter do not exist. Prof. Issel does not agree with M. Rivière in thinking that figures on the dolmens and menhirs in Europe have no resemblance to ours, for though they are not cut in the same way, he notes the circles, spirals, curved shapes like the letter U, that is two horns without a body, and figures of men and axes with or without handles, all of which we have.

Prof. Lissauer of Berlin attributes the figures to the Iberian branch of the Mediterranean family. These as well as ancient Ligurians, Pelasgians, and Etruscans, are generally believed to have been of the same stock and of north African origin. If these figures had been cut in modern times, we might perhaps be able to say from what countries the people might have come, for oxen are not yoked in the same way in all of them. Senor de Aranzadi, in an interesting pamphlet on the subject, says that in Asia, Africa except part of Barbary, half of eastern Europe, and Italy, they are yoked by the neck, as are evidently the oxen of the figures on our rocks; whereas in Spain except Galicia and Catalonia, in France, Switzerland, Austria, etc. they are yoked by the horns; so that if the customs were the same in early times as now, our sculptors would more probably have come from Italy than from France or Spain.

As, unfortunately, no discoveries of human remains have as yet been made in our mountains, we have no direct evidence to help us in our speculations. Some of the men who engraved the rocks must have died there in the summer months, and their tombs may yet be discovered, or their weapons, or other things which will throw light upon the subject. In the hope of finding some sign or other of their presence we have dug at various times in different places, at the foot of rocks most abundantly scored with figures, in a rock shelter in the Fontanalba valley, and in a cave near the mines, where we thought we might perhaps find remains of tools with which they worked, but we have found nothing. We have seen no indications which might denote burial places. We have sometimes thought of trying where there are very ancient circles of stones now hardly noticeable, but the work would be very long and arduous, and we have been loth to give up a day's useful work for one of sheer hard manual labour with so little hope of reward. One friend believes that the sculptors probably threw votive offerings of weapons into the lakes, and especially into the Lago Agnel, but naturally we cannot dredge in these.

For the present then we can only say that the authors of the engravings were at least in part an agricultural people who possessed weapons some of which are believed to be those of the early bronze period, perhaps 1000-1500 B. C., although it is possible that in the mountain region the tribes who dwelt there were still using bronze when those on the coast or in the plains had iron ones. There can be no doubt about the great antiquity of the figures. The forms represented, the appearance of the engravings in comparison with those of some centuries ago, the depth below the present level of the ground at which many are found, prove it. There were certainly tribes in Phoenician as well as in Roman times dwelling in the mountains and hard to conquer. They may have been established there, or have fled into the fastnesses of the high country from invading enemies. Prof. Issel says that the forms of the engraved weapons do not correspond with those characteristic ones from the valley of the Po, but have greater affinity with those from southern France, and especially from the plains along the banks of the Rhone. He therefore concludes that as those plains were inhabited by Iberians who had relations with the inhabitants of Algeria and Morocco, and as moreover some of the weapon figures in Fontanalba represent a type of scythe common to western Europe, Ireland, France, Sardinia and Iberian lands, our sculptors probably came from the Rhone Valley where Iberians and Celts intermingled, and from there may have made long pilgrimages to the rocks of the Maritime Alps. The human figures are represented naked, which would suggest that they came from warm countries, and the figures of the ploughs that they lived in the plains. Were it not for this unanswerable argument of the weapons, we certainly should have thought it more probable that they came from the Italian plains than from the seacoast. The routes by the Roja or the Vesubie valley would have been much more difficult than that by the Vermegnana valley to the north of the Col di Tenda. Where Tenda now stands would have been then as now a good centre for a pastoral colony, and when there was not sufficient pasture there it would have been easy in the summer months to ascend to the Miniera and Casterino valleys. If they came with herds they would surely never have ascended the long Gordolasca valley and crossed the high and rocky Passo Arpeto. There would have been abundant pasture lower down, and at least in historic times our regions have only been approached by way of the Miniera or Sabbione valleys. If they lived far away from the rocks, that is to say were not as near as Val Casterino and the Miniera, but came over from the French side, we ask why they did not leave more records on all those smooth and coloured rocks so near the pass, instead of going much farther on down to the lakes, and even across more passes into the Fontanalba valley? We cannot help thinking also that the engravings in the lower parts of the valleys, those around the Laghi Lunghi and near Lago Verde, so many of which are rudely done and have large deep holes, are among the earliest ones, while those higher up show signs of progress both in designs and in workmanship. We had never thought that the people could have lived so far off as the valley of the Rhone and made such long journeys to reach the Maritime Alps, nor can we conceive how they could have discovered such places unless they were quartered near, but we can well admit that they originally came from the west but were afterwards established in our mountains. We think that people living in those days as far north as southern France could not have lived unclothed, and that the figures are for the most part drawn naked only the better to show that they indicate men. The whole question, who were these people and whence did they come, is a very difficult and mysterious one, and for the present we have not sufficient data to be able to arrive at any very satisfactory conclusion. Till lately we had always understood that the remains of a man who was found dead in the valley were lying just where our cottage stands, but as he was not a prehistoric one we had no desire to disturb his bones. We now know that these remains were exhumed and taken down to Tenda, but if the spirits of the prehistoric people are still existing, perhaps they have inspired us to settle where they did once, and we have spent so many years in thinking about them and their works that we have done our best to give them an immortality in this world.

There are other difficult problems to solve besides that of the race of people. One is, how long did the practice of cutting figures continue? Prof. Issel thinks that the sculptors were probably few in number, and went many times but few together during a series of years, certainly during more than a century. Unless they went in large numbers and only for the purpose of cutting figures it would have taken them a very long time. But we cannot understand people continuing this occupation the whole summer, and believe that they only went at some particular time in the summer on pilgrimages of short duration. Pastoral people would not have lived long so far away from their homes and occupations, and maintained themselves only by what wild game they could procure. Mr Moggridge says that in some parts of India the natives go up to the mountain heights when the snow has melted, and carve upon the rocks mystic signs as a notification to posterity. Why should people have gone up to such inhospitable regions as ours? One cannot help thinking that the valleys below could not have been much populated by agricultural people, and there were regions all around much more attractive than the wild and rocky ones covered by snow the greater part of the year. If cowherds, goatherds and shepherds ever frequented these places even in greater numbers than now, could they have devoted much time to engraving the rocks, and even supposing that it became a

PLATE XXVI.

Figures in the 'Via Sacra,' Val Fontanalba.

favourite summer duty or pastime, and that each succeeding year the people imitated their predecessors or continued their own amusement of the year before, how could they have cut so many? Let us try to realize for a moment the Fontanalba region with its 70C0 figures more or less covering many square kilometres of savage mountain sides. Can we conceive it possible that day after day in the short summer months people would have found any amusement in cutting these figures, some of which are so large that many hours, possibly days, would have been needed to finish them? In the present day when the sheep or goats are feeding, their masters lie down and sleep or do nothing. When their herds are moving they must be on the move also, driving them in the direction of those places where there is a little grass, keeping them together, and preventing them from straying and getting lost to sight above the cliffs or down in the innumerable gullies and ravines. And how can we imagine that people took their flocks to so many places where there is the most rock and the least pasture, in fact to so many places where now we never see them? As we have said we now see the goats going up to the top of M. S. Maria where there are no figures, and the sheep generally lower down in more grassy places where there are few. If there were only a few people there in the old days, and if they were not extraordinarily different in their habits from those of the present day, the figures would not have been cut in a century. We are inclined to think that many people must have gone there together and even then during a long series of years, but only for a very short time, and that they were not engaged when there in any other occupation, but went for the express purpose of cutting the figures.

As we do not know when and whence they came so we do not know why and when they left. Perhaps they were driven away by enemies. They certainly did not leave because there were no more rocks to decorate, for there are still whole regions where there is not a single mark and where those who pass by now have not left even a scratch. We often wonder both in the Fontanalba and the Meraviglie regions why so many of the smoothest and most brilliant red and yellow surfaces have received either few engravings or none. Nevertheless these places are not like many other known ones where one particular spot or a few rocks near together have been chosen to record the names or other signs of the visitors, or like any modern place of pilgrimage with one special centre of attraction. The whole Fontanalba valley from the Paracuerta lake to the Monte Bego scree, and the Valauretta valley, and the vast tract beyond the high crest of M. Bego right away to the Passo Arpeto have all been a place of pilgrimage. Why was this a sort of sanctuary? Was it only the brighly coloured rock which attracted the sculptors, or was there some fascination about the culminating and storm-brewing mountain and its deity, as M. Blanc suggests? Apparently the Fontanalba people did not go over to the Meraviglie region or into Val Valauretta, or they would have left their special sign-manuals there, for, as we have said, the figures though much alike in each of the regions have in each some particular types in large numbers. They must have discovered these extraordinary rocks, and then made use of them as being specially adapted for whatever they wished to record. We have said in an earlier pamphlet that we did think Monte Bego was a special attraction to them with its rugged shape, its great cliffs and precipices, its triangular summit and its stormy character, and though we have lately found a few figures far away under Col Sabbione, we do not think that we need altogether give up that idea. The whole country round it may have been a kind of sanctuary and place of pilgrimage, and the strangely coloured rocks so unlike any others were as the walls round an ancient temple or a modern shrine upon which are hung the offerings and records of the faithful. "Great is Diana of the Ephesians" the people cried out for the space of two hours when the silversmiths of Ephesus were afraid that Paul's preaching might diminish the sale of the little images which the pilgrims bought at the shrine "where all Asia and the world worshipped;" And great may have been Monte Bego among the surrounding peaks to these primitive and superstitious people. Every time we have walked up the Val Fontanalba and seen its snowy crest or purple precipices illuminated by the first rays of sunshine in the early morning, we have been impressed by the beauty of the scene; and every time we

PLATE XXVII.

1. 2. Rocks near the upper Margheria, Val Fontanalba.

have been to the Meraviglie lake, and looked at the glaciated rocks
in the middle of the chaos and ruin all around, and at the pinnacles
some of which Dr Henry said seemed almost to have been cut
by human hands, we have 'wondered': and if in the prehistoric days
there were thicker forests below and the Ciappe of Fontanalba and
the Meraviglie were still smoother and brighter and less furrowed
by grass, they would have been even more astonishing than they
are now, and we can understand that people would have gone
from far away to make their records and leave their vows.

Prof. Issel says that the figures:

1. May have been intended to perpetuate the memory of a
mysterious cult or of sacrifice offered to the divinity.

2. May have been in a certain manner the archives to keep the
records of memorable events, such as of victories won, peace or
truces concluded, quarrels adjusted, administrative and political
arrangements, alliances and marriages.

3. May have had for their scope the determination of bounda-
ries of properties belonging to different tribes or peoples, or to
define rights of property or pasture, or were in some manner
treaties and decisions which were meant to resolve the questions
between peoples or tribes.

and 4. That the registration in these alpine valleys of these
administrative or historical documents may have taken place in a
solemn manner, and been accompanied by religious ceremonies to
implore the favour of the divinity, whose seat, as among other
peoples and in other countries, was believed to be in the lofty
mountains.

He also says " The long and wearisome work necessary
to make these figures, the climatic conditions, the wildness and
barrenness of the place, are a clear proof that the sculptors attributed great importance to their work, and that they chose these
difficult and remote regions far from their habitual habitations to
preserve it from desecration and possibly to hide it from the vain
curiosity of others." If they did have this object in view they
would have been like the Egyptians burying their dead in the hidden
recesses of the wadys near Luxor, or sealing them up in the
mysterious chambers of the pyramids or deep down in the desert

sands, to preserve them not only from profanation but also from the vulgar gaze. With the Professor's conclusions we are almost entirely in agreement, and believe that the figures, whether singly or in combinations, had meanings. The single ones may have indicated the occupation of those who cut them, such as herdsmen, agriculturalists, hunters etc., or were marks to denote their tribe or family like the totem marks in America, or were their own particular marks, their picture signatures.

We would also suggest some other interpretations. As the figures on so many rocks do not seem to be in any way grouped, and are often only figures of horns, and as there are also many rocks where there is only one single figure, it seems to us that the figures may merely have been a record of their visit, an offering made at the sanctuary, which would be equivalent to that of a candle or a silver heart, which are the commonest forms of offerings in these days, at least at Christian shrines. If apart from the signing of contrasts or recording events, their pilgrimages to the high places had, as we believe, a religious idea, then everyone would have deemed it necessary to carve his mark whether the mark had any symbolic meaning or not. It was his gift, or his prayer, or at least the record that he had come there, and it was " graven with an iron pen ", as it were, " on the rock for ever." Our friend A. Dolsa wrote " I have made this lion," and the prehistoric people meant to say " I have cut this beast, this weapon, this circle etc." For countless ages people have been going on pilgrimage, people of all nations and countries and creeds, and though many are today quite as superstitious as any prehistoric ones ever could have been, there is no doubt that in early times everybody was so, and customs were practised and charms and amulets used to ward off all kinds of evils that might be inflicted by visible or invisible enemies. It is not necessary to believe that there was anything specially sacred about Monte Bego, or that a divinity had his seat there. Those coloured rocks were their archives, their Jerusalem or Mecca, and they went there to engrave something somewhere, one man perhaps joining with his fellows in making a record together, and another going off by himself to some more remote and secret corner, and making his offering alone, but each one hoping to get some benefit by so doing. The figures of ploughs,

of horns, of huts, or of weapons, might have been the prayer for
good seasons, increase of flocks and herds, good luck to his house
and family or success in the chase, and all the others protection
for himself.

Another suggestion is that as the horns are everywhere except
in Val Valauretta, and comprise more than half of the entire number of the engravings, these horns had some particular value. The
horn cut in the middle of the breast of the large human figure in
the Vallone delle Meraviglie must surely be of great importance.
There is not any doubt that in many countries horns have been
the symbols of power and then of protection. Horns, crests, plumes
upon the head of beast or bird were conspicuous marks of might
and superiority, and presently men began to decorate themselves
with them. They are to be seen on the heads of Egyptian and
Greek divinities. They are spoken of in ancient Hebrew writings,
and were an ornament of Jewish altars. They were put upon ancient helmets and they are found on Etruscan tombs, and in one
form or another they are common amulets even today. Even the
children here in Bordighera make the sign of two horns when a
companion is cruel or malicious. They both protect themselves
and probably wish something evil to their neighbour at the same
time. The Christian Church has put them on the head of Moses,
believing that he came down from the mountain with this symbol
of authority, and this curious prayer is used at the consecration of
a Roman Catholic bishop " We set on the head of this bishop, O
Lord, Thy champion, the helmet of defence and salvation, that with
comely face and with his head armed with the horns of either
testament he may appear terrible to the gainsayers of the truth,
and may become their vigorous assailant, through the abundant
gift of Thy grace, Who didst make the face of Thy servant Moses
to shine after familiar converse with Thee, and didst adorn it
with the resplendent horns of Thy brightness and truth etc." Horns
are also often hung over the doors of houses and elsewhere to
keep off evil spirits. As the devil is popularly supposed to have
the terrifying horns, this is paying him back in his own coin.
These innumerable figures of horns on the rocks may then have
had some of these meanings, and were not only in some cases

the picture, and in others the symbol of an ox which was the people's most valuable possession, but may have been a sort of religious symbol to ensure good luck and protect from bad. Were this a true interpretation of these numerous figures, we should have an explanation of the very astonishing variety of the forms which the sculptors invented, and in drawing which they certainly showed considerable artistic gifts. It could not have been at all easy to cut some of them so symmetrically, or to keep the fine lines so even by a multitude of little round holes, but if they put their whole heart into the work on account of its important character, they took pains to do it well, and a new form of horns or a pair of immense size out of all proportion to the figure either of head or body, would have been the equivalent of a very long or a very florid prayer such as one may see in devotional books. They too like many others may have hoped to be the more heard " for their much speaking." We may also ask why was a horn so often cut touching or across another figure? We can understand the horn inside an enclosing square or circle, as representing the possession of cattle, but if it be cut across a weapon or fixed to its points, or drawn across the contour of an enclosure, we must suppose it to have been an important addition meaning something more. If it were not for Val Valauretta without even one horned figure, we might say that whatever else anyone cut he certainly cut a horn as well. It is possible that some of the forms to which we can assign no interpretation may not have had one, and may only have been new and beautiful figures as more important memorials, longer and more fervent prayers, more costly offerings.

One other interpretation of the engravings, slightly different to the above, is perhaps worthy of consideration. The sculptors symbolically sacrificed the best of their possession, giving a picture of it instead of the thing itself. A not very clever divinity might not recognize the difference, and a kind one might be expected to be content with the second best. Anyhow though prophets have always rightly preached that a good heart and a good life are more important than all outward gifts and cere-monies, the idea of sacrificing something has always been the popular one.

PLATE XXVIII.

The 'Ciappe di Fontanalba.'
1. From Lago Verde. 2. From the small lakes above Lago Verde.

PLATE XXIX.

Rock on 'Skin Hill,' Val Fontanalba.

CHAPTER VII.

Guide to Val Fontanalba.

The following pages are a guide to the Fontanalba region, and will be of little interest to general readers, but as there is not sufficient detail in any of the maps to make them of much use to future visitors with little time to spare, we hope these notes may be of some service to them, and prevent them from wandering about in the valley as Prof. Celesia did to little purpose. We can describe certain landmarks which fairly well divide the region into natural parts, and we shall mention these in order, and point out some of the figures most worth seeing. The plates give some of the most interesting ones, both single figures and groups of them.

1. *The eastern hillside above the lower part of the valley.*

a) If we ascend Val Fontanalba by the right bank we reach in twenty minutes an open meadow, and see across the valley the steep hillside under the crest which eventually culminates in Monte Santa Maria. A spur at right angles to this crest runs across the valley from north to south farther on. A little part of the higher rocks of the Ciappe di Fontanalba is visible beyond this spur, and the cliffs and summit of Monte Bego. The crest mentioned ends to the east just above a small lake marked on the maps as Lago di Fontanalba, but which the shepherds who know the old names much better than those who have made the maps, more rightly call Lago di Paracuerta, giving the former name to the highest lake from which the Fontanalba stream flows. On the hillside, a little north of where one looks down on the Paracuerta lake, are a few figures, the nearest to Val Casterino, but it is difficult to find them and impossible to explain to others. There are many smooth yellow rocks above and near the lake, and many more on the open land between the river and the foot of the steep slopes, but we have found no figures there.

b) Farther west than those just mentioned are a good many figured rocks near together, and we can easily make out their position, for looking up at the hillside from the lower meadow, we cannot help noticing near the highest larches a flat diamond-shaped surface, looking much smoother than anything else near it, and which shines more brightly in the afternoon light. On the direct way up to this, a little below to the east, are many smoothish but dark surfaces, on which if we look carefully are to be found about fifty figures, including two with double horns (Pl. VIII. 7). At the top of these are some smoother coloured rocks with an excellent plough (Pl. III. 1) some horns with loops (Pl. XXV. 3) and others, in all about 30 figures. (Pl. XXV. 1-10). A hundred metres higher up is the diamond-shaped rock. This has a very curious double-horned figure with bar across it and a group of rectangular ones with straight lines (Pl. XVIII. 23).

c) The next figured rocks on this hillside are reached by continuing along the hillside almost horizontally, or by ascending from the meadow where is the middle Margheria. On the north side of this meadow are many parallel rock-ridges running down to the valley, towards the top of which are several smooth surfaces with about 60 figures. (Pl. XXV. 11-16). Here Prof. Celesia copied some. There are also a few in the gullies between the ridges. At this spot the buttress which runs across the valley originates. The figures are mostly horns of various forms, some skins, two ploughs, one with man and one of the oxen either unfinished or worn away, one figure of a man with implement, a U form, and a circle with two diameters in the form of a cross and with five short parallel lines below. This Prof. Issel thinks has some numerical signification (Pl. XXV. 13).

2. *The spur crossing the valley.*

a) In the middle of this spur is a narrow gully or valley which comes down from the S. Maria crest to the Fontanalba stream. This is the Valletta di Santa Maria. There are only a few very bad and worn figures in it.

b) The steep banks on the west are chiefly composed of scree and rough schist surfaces, with figures here and there on the best of them (Pl. XXV. 17-19) except towards the top where there are more. One group is near the upper Margheria, and easily found as the rock is of such a brilliant colour. (Pl. XXV. 20).

Others are farther north at the bottom of grassy slopes which lead up to two small lakes. Here are many figures of implements, plans of huts or rocks with enclosures, horns, etc. (Pl. XXV. 21-25).

c) The most important engraved surface north of the last is a long bank of red rock, perhaps some 50 metres in length, with narrow grass slope between it and the rock wall on the other side. This we called on the first year of our explorations the '*Via Sacra,*' fancying that it was a sort of natural passage from the meadows below up into the heart of the engraved regions, and also because it is a reward to anyone who has climbed the long steep scree above the meadow of the Margheria under a broiling sun. If one does this, one reaches the Valletta di Santa Maria, crosses it, and the Via Sacra is just opposite above the valley cliff. Here Prof. Celesia found the figure of the ' man with uplifted arms.' There are about 130 figures in all along this surface, two ploughs with men and one without, a man holding an implement, a small human figure, an axe, many curious shapes of horns, some triangular arrow or spear heads, many geometrical figures and interesting properties with spots inside and outside them (Pl. XXV. 26-38), also a large figure given not very correctly by Celesia, which at first sight seems to represent two beetles crawling up a stick, but which may possibly represent skins hung out to dry, though the resemblance is not very great, and it is better to assign it to the class of incomprehensible figures (Pl. XXV. 39). All these figures are on the eastern side of the culminating ridge of the spur. Other parts of this spur must be described separately, that is the regions north of Lago Verde as far as the two small lakes.

d) The upper Margheria consists of a few broken-down huts above Lago Verde, A path up the left bank of Val Fontanalba leads to them, and continues horizontally under the south end of the spur and then turns north into a marshy valley west of it. Above the lake and on both sides of this path and close to the Margheria are many figures, some very deeply cut and of the skin pattern. (Pl. XX. 21-22 and XXV. 40-42). Here is a loose rock engraved with 30 figures including a plough, some rectangles and enclosures, and many horns. (Pl. XXVII. 1). Many of the figures on these rocks have a very archaic look and the holes are large and deep.

e) Close to the Margheria is a small pond, full of tadpoles in the early summer, but generally quite dried up by the end of August. A rock partly in the water is engraved, and in the little valley beyond the pond and on the hillside crowned with larches, almost as far as the two lakes, are figures. Above the pond and near the Margheria is a rock with arrow-heads and a four-horned figure (Pl. VIII. 9); also one which we call the ' *Baby Rock,* ' as all the figures are cut on a very small scale. (Pl. XXV. 49-51). It takes a long time to explore all this neighbourhood, for there are so many little rocks just above the grass which have roughly cut figures on any polished part, but which can only be seen by careful search (Pl. XXV. 44-49 and XLIV. 2). From the two little lakes farther on and from Lago Verde are the best views of the Ciappe di Fontanalba, the great ice-worn central white mass of rock. (Pl. XXVII. 1, 2). By the side of the lower lake are worn figures and two or three on the slopes towards the marshy valley.

3. *The marshy valley.*

This lies between the above-described spur and the foot of the central mass. In a few places one can climb on to the latter but along the greater part of the valley the rock wall is too steep and high. The stream from the highest Fontanalba lake flows through this valley and there is much boggy ground white with cotton-grass in the summer. In the middle of it is an abandoned ' gias ' or goat-shed, and close to this the water passes between some rocks covered with figures including some interesting looped ones, skins and others. (Pl. XX. 13 and XXX. 1-5). Other rocks near and beyond are also covered but the figures are mostly nearly worn away. In all there are about 60 figures in the marshy valley. At the head of it there is one of the old enclosures formed by a big rock and the remains of a rectangular wall.

PLATE XXX.

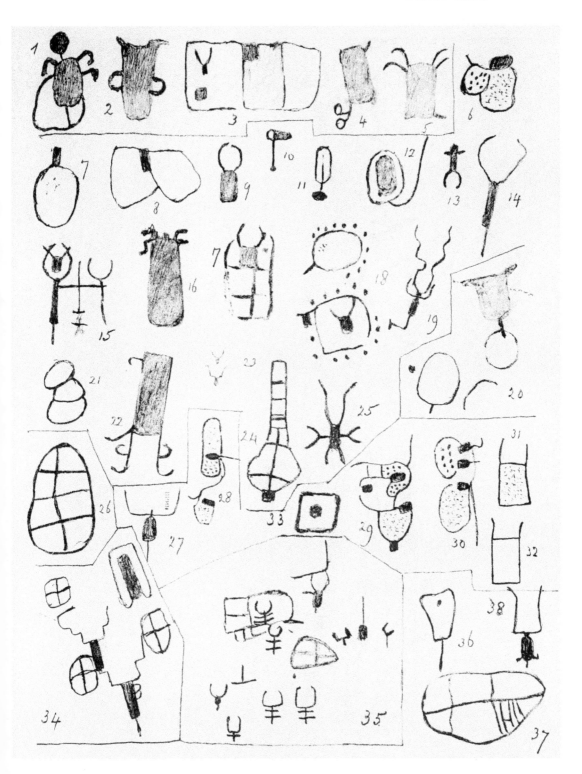

Figures in Val Fontanalba *(continued)*.

PLATE XXXI.

The great red Santa Maria rock, Val Fontanalba.

4. *Skin Hill.*

We are now face to face with the steep hillsides of M. S. Maria. The stream flows down between the white central mass and the much greyer hillside in front of us. This grey part as far as where the whiter and yellower rocks begin on the left bank of the stream we call '*Skin Hill,*' because one of the first coloured surfaces a little way up the hill is covered with skin figures. There are a few figures to the east of this ascent in a little valley which joins the Valletta di S. Maria much higher up. Many red rocks on Skin hill, one above the other, are very clearly seen from the marshy valley. Near the stream at the lower part is a very good specimen of a collection of figured huts or properties, which we call the '*Skin Hill Village*' (Pl. XLIII. 4). At the beginning of the ascent are worn figured rocks, then comes the one with the many skins, then another with figure like a skin but with loop above it and spots all round (Pl. XX. 1-7) and a man. These two rocks have each about 25 figures. Then, still ascending, we reach a rock with ploughs and men, ard two yoked horned figures of very unequal dimensions (Pl. III. 15). One horned figure is curious as the head is so like a weapon. (Pl. VII. 26). Another red surface more to the left has nearly 100 figures in great confusion, among them some enclosures with spots all round (Pl. XXX. 18 XLIV. 4 and XLV. 2) and another double surface · more to the east, where water generally flows down, has a number of figures forming a complete picture. Considerably higher up the hill we come to two rocks, one the '*Butterfly Rock*' with three figures looking somewhat like huge butterflies, a plough etc., (Pl. XX. 15, 16) and another close by '*The Looped Skin Rock*' (Pl. XXIX). This is a beautifully smooth and nearly vertical surface, one of the easiest to photograph, with 40-50 figures including the looped skin (Pl. XX. 12), a plough, a man with weapon etc., and on the continuation of the same rock wall are very small and delicately cut figures. Not far from the Butterfly rock is a gully to the east in which is a large figure, the only one of the kind in the whole region (Pl. XX. 14). When after a farther ascent we again approach the stream, just above it and overlooking some brilliant red rocks on the opposite side is a rock with the figures of Pl. XXX. 24 and VII. 52 and a strange one not far off (Pl. XXX. 25). There are many other rocks scattered about on Skin hill with one or more figures on them, and there are some nearer to the steeper part of the mountain, but those we have mentioned are the principal ones. There are about 450 figures in all. (Pl. XXX. 6-25). Just above where a small stream from the north joins the main one, the grey rocks come to an end, and a series of more coloured or whiter ones begins. All this higher region on the left bank of the stream up to the higher lake and the ridge of M. S. Maria we call the *Santa Maria Rocks.*

5. *The Santa Maria Rocks.*

a) At the foot near the stream are some rough rocks with very large conspicuous figures including a huge circle with two diameters, and an oblong with eight bars across it. The ground here is level and there is a small pond; above it rises steeply. (Pl. XVIII. 10 and XXX. 26).

b) To the north is a narrow strip of rock with steep face towards M. S. Maria and a narrow gully on the south, the first ridge. At the lower part are horned figures and properties. Near the top where it becomes very narrow and the gully ends, are beautiful smooth surfaces with large geometrical figures and complex ones, with two of the skin type on a ledge just above the gully, one only outlined, the other with spots inside, apparently a not well-finished engraving. This ridge has 140 figures (Pl. XXX. 27-34).

c) The second ridge to the south joins this last one at the top and is bounded by another gully leading down to near the stream. It has 80 figures. At the bottom is a surface with large rectangular figures and others, (Pl. XLIV. 5), apparently a connected group. Higher up is a rock with the very white modern date 1795, four horned figures perhaps symbols of oxen, with horns, body, and legs denoted by lines of equal thickness, and others. This is a good specimen of a rock with different sorts of figures cut by diverse hands (Pl. XXX. 35 and 36-38). On rocks above are many small implements etc.

d) The third ridge is much larger, runs up the slopes much farther, and is bounded by a ravine of considerable depth which joins the stream some hundred metres above the foot of the Santa Maria Rocks. The surfaces of greatest interest are two close together and near where the first and second ridges unite. These, covered with figures, are the ones we have mentioned which we discovered late one September afternoon when the sun, low in the sky, cast more shadow and brought to light all the figures which we had so often passed before but not observed. One, the '*September Rock*' has a very elaborate series of enclosures with the large and small spots etc., and the other has five figures of men, also a plough, a harrow, etc. On this ridge are many figures of ploughs with men, a very large oblong one with divisions, etc. (Pl. XXXII 1-3). Towards the top the ridge is more or less level and unites with the fourth ridge. On this upper part are many very interesting things, a circle with long handle, some zigzag horns united, a unique enclosure with parallelogram and two kinds of spots inside, the figure with weapon cut across it at a later date, and others. (Pl. VII. 50, IX. 26, XVIII. 33, 34 and XXXII. 4). There are 120 figures on this ridge.

e) The fourth ridge beyond the ravine has only a few figures on the lower part, chiefly near the stream, and there is no distinguishing mark to show exactly where it ends.

f) The great red Santa Maria rock.

This is the magnificent steep slope which faces us at the top of the third ridge. (Pl. XXXI). It is perhaps 100 metres long, and is one of the most astonishing coloured and glaciated surfaces in the whole region. There are probably about 300 figures on it, many of them of immense size. The largest horned figure is here, measuring 316×99c., also the great enclosure with 86 beasts, also ploughs, weapons, and all sorts of types. (Pl. XLV. 3, XX. 19, 20, XXXII. 5-12, also VIII. 13. 39, IX. 12, 27, etc.). It must be visited often and especially towards evening if one would see all the figures. With the exception of the large complex figures, and a few others, the engravings on this rock do not seem to be divided into groups.

g) On the rocks to the left or south of this great surface there is not much. Quite at the bottom by a long grassy glade are some groups of interlacing horns (Pl. XLV. 3). On the higher parts and near the great lake there are a few figures, and also a few nearer the crest of S. Maria. There are many slopes of very brilliant colour, but we have explored them often without much success. The highest figure, a single horn, is close to the ridge near Cima Bicknell at over 2600 m.

6. *The Great Central Mass.*

Some parts of this can easily be described and found, but we are unable to say much about the larger part of it in the centre, as there are no very clear landmarks there, and though we have spent so many days upon it, we do not yet know it thoroughly, and are not able to locate a good many of the figures. The whole region, which is itself most clearly marked off from the surrounding ones, is bounded by the stream from the upper lake, and by the cliff of what we call the '*Great Gully.*' This gully and cliff are very well seen from Lago Verde. The lower part of the central mass, as we have already explained, is the rock wall above the marshy valley, and the whole of it is the most striking part of the rock region of Fontanalba.

a) *The Castle Rock ridge.*

This is a well defined ridge most to the north above the right bank of the stream. On the south side for part of its length is a high cliff. If we cross the stream just below the top of Skin Hill, we see several smooth red rocks one above the other, and which are very visible from the marshy valley. The lowest we call '*Armour Rock*' with many weapon figures. (Pl. XXXII. 13). Next above it is '*Fork Rock*' also with weapons, one with loop or strap attached to it, a very large horned figure nearly a metre long and broad, very many horned figures like forks including four yoked together, and many large geometrical figures. (Pl. XXXII. 15, XIII. 15, VII. 25 and III. 25). Above this is a surface with large squares and circles, and above this again are two which we call '*Castle Rock*' and '*Lobster Rock.*' On the first is a long rectangular figure (Pl. XXXII. 16) faintly suggesting the castle tower of the chessmen; on the other some curious horns two of which on our first visit

PLATE XXXII.

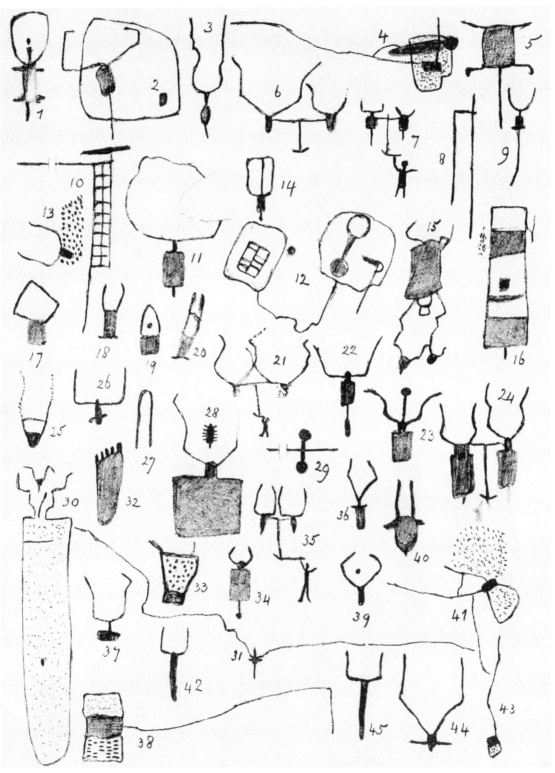

Figures in Val Fontanalba *(continued)*.

PLATE XXXIII.

Two views of the upper large smooth surface, Val Fontanalba.

appeared to us to be something like crustaceans, lobsters or scorpions with large claws. (Pl. VIII. 42). Another large horned figure close by is curious (Pl. IX. 28). By the little ravine just south of these rocks is a good figure of a plough with four yoked beasts. Higher up on this ridge are many figures (Pl. IX. 16, XXXII. 17, XLIV. 1) chiefly horns. One rock has a curious group, part of which is evidently a complete design, but the other part was not cut by the same person. In this are two beasts facing one another with spots outside which we take to represent eyes. They seem to be an affectionate pair gazing at each other. Close to these is a very good example of three horned figures of different sizes symmetrically arranged in a vertical line. Below, close to the stream and opposite the ravine of the S. Maria rocks are several smooth surfaces with good figures (Pl. XXXII. 18-21, XLIII. 1). Of one we have spoken before. The plough figure is interesting because the oxen have the side appendages which must represent their legs. Other ploughs are on rocks close by. A little above this are some small ponds through which the stream passes, and here another gentle ascent begins and continues to the upper lake.

b) *Elephant Gully and neighbourhood.*

There is a well-defined region beginning at these ponds which comprises all the upper part of the central mass bounded on three sides by the stream, the big lake, and the great cliff of the big gully. At the lower part, not far from the ponds, are many rocks with figures, These are in the direction of the cliff. The nearest one is in a small gully, the figures cut on a rough anagenite surface, and we call it the '*Elephant Rock*' on account of the large figures there. One plough measures 58c. $\times$ 52c.: another has an ox with knob at the end of its tail almost as large as the ploughman (Pl. XXXII. 22-24, III. 7).

There are other figures beyond towards the cliff, and on the way up to the lake is a figure of weapon or implement with four rivets denoted at the bottom of the blade and two outside (Pl. XII. 23). Just above the head of the lake are a few weapons and other figures (Pl. XXXII. 25, 26) and there are figures in a kind of alley above and parallel with the cliff.

c) *The Big Beast Gully.*

This is south of the Castle Rock ridge below its high cliff. There is one good surface low down and there are many towards the top. (Pl. XXXII. 27-30, VII. 23, IX. 29, XIII. 76). Here is the second largest horned figure 177c $\times$ 59c., and which gave the name to this gully, but we have since seen the still longer one on the S. Maria rocks. There is also the one with horizontal horns measuring 259c. from tip to tip and the curious enclosure with spots, partly broken, and which gives the idea of a sheepfold with barrier inside near the entrance as if to allow the animals to be counted on entering it. (Pl. XXXII. 30-31). On a rock near are the largest human figure 19c. $\times$ 11c., a strange pair of horns, and just below many geometrical figures. There are in this gully about 70 figures. One at the top like a dumbbell with bar across it is the only one of the kind. This gully does not quite reach the marshy valley, but just below the end of it is a rock with a very large skin, a harrow, and other figures (Pl. XXXIV. 18), and another with a strange engraving the greater part of which was underground (Pl. XXXIV. 17).

d) *The Middle large smooth surface.*

Near the head of the Big Beast Gully is the middle one of the three large smoothest surfaces of the central mass. These, with the exception of the great red rock under M. S. Maria, are the largest, smoothest and most striking of all those in Val Fontanalba. This middle one has some of the most remarkable horned figures, in great variety of shape and very little resembling oxen or other beasts. (VII. 21, IX. 33). Here is the best figure of a plough with three men (III. 10), a weapon with two rings at the end of the handle (XIII. 18) a triangular one with open handle, an enclosure with smaller one within it (XVIII. 35), and yoked horns of the fork pattern. (III. 27). Except for the change of colour these figures seem hardly to have deteriorated since they were cut, and many are done with great skill. Only the two large horned figures, near the northern end of the rock, with immense zigzag horns, are to be found with difficulty as they are badly injured. There are on this surface about 34 figures.

PLATE XXXIV.

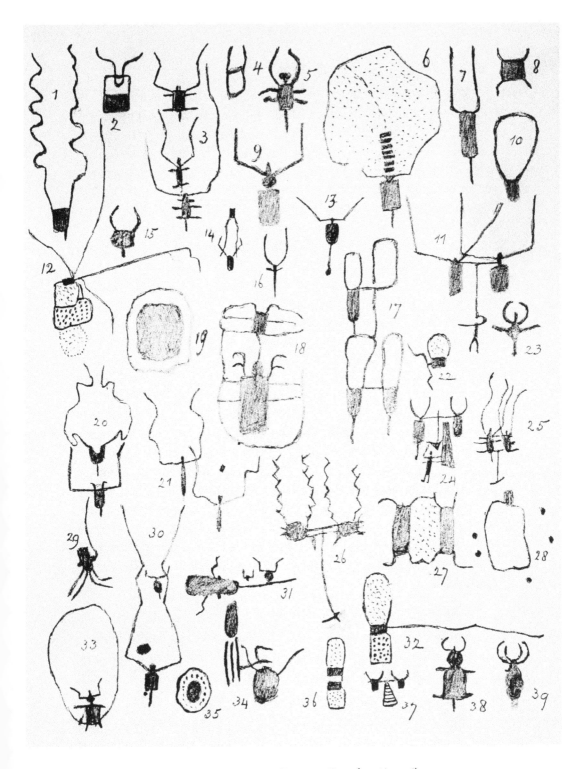

Figures in Val Fontanalba *(continued).*

e) *The Upper large smooth surface.*

This is quite close to the last and directly above it. It is undoubtedly the finest surface of all and should not be missed by anyone who has time and energy to climb a good deal higher than the figured rocks near Lago Verde. We have been in the habit of taking visitors to what we call the '*300 Rock*' on account of the quantity and variety of figures on it all close together, but this immense surface which except for its red and yellow colour is for all the world like a piece of a glacier, is probably still more worth seeing (Pl. XXXIII.) The upper and lower parts have many figures, and there are naturally a great many of very large size, for the sculptors had full room to display their talents and fancies. There are 175 figures in all, that is if we have managed to find them all. We tried to do this, marking each one by a small stone which was thrown away when our rubbing was completed. On this surface is the best figure of the weapon which has been called a halberd, very well cut (Pl. XIII. 26 and XIV. 1) and what seems to be a scythe (XIII. 25) the long horns (VII. 13, 15, 24), the strange figure (IX. 30) and two figures one of which (XXXII. 38) has one long line attached to it, and the other one two lines. Also near the bottom of the rock is a figure of a foot, a unique engraving (Pl. XXXII. 32). It is evident that the sculptor placed his bare foot on the rock and then drew the outline round it before cutting it out. It measures 28c. $\times$ 14c. I find my own foot is 27c. $\times$ 10 $^1/_2$ c. There are about 180 figures here, but there do not seem to be any recognizable groups. Below the upper side of this great surface are lovely smooth and yellow rocks almost untouched.

f) *The Lower large smooth surface.*

This is somewhat lower down to the south and has 46 figures, weapons, skins, and many large horns, but there is nothing very remarkable except the character of the rock itself (Pl. XXXII. 42-45).

g) *The main part of the central mass.*

We cannot well explain the position of most of the figures here. A few are shown in Plate XXXIV. 1-16. Of these N. 2 and

N. 6 are interesting, especially the latter, a horned figure, the horns joining to form a circle, and within them a row of seven little parallelograms and a quantity of dots. On a smooth surface somewhat difficult of access just above the wall of the marshy valley are some very large circles. A strip a long way above this and parallel with the Big Beast gully, is rich in figures. Here are, or at least were, the two figures of Plate XVIII. 18, 19., but the latter is now in the Bordighera museum. We had copied it the very first year of our explorations and then were unable to find it again, though we knew more or less whereabouts it was. When after ten years search we again found it, we noticed that the part of the rock on which it was cut was loose, and with the help of two friends worked the whole day and were able to cut away a large part outside the figure to lighten its weight, and then with considerable difficulty and great fatigue for three hours to carry it down home. There are also many figures near a loose block in about the centre of the mass, and which has reached its present position since the days of the sculptors, for there are many figures underneath it. Between this block and the cliff of the great gully figures are fairly abundant. Those of Plate IX. 12 and XVIII. 37 are there.

h) *The south east corner of the central mass.*

This is a small well-defined region with over 90 figures. On the north of it is a deep cutting in the rock with vertical walls, in which are two figures. This is the '*Closed Gully,*' and a little beyond is another similar cutting but much larger and with a single larch tree in it, '*One-tree Gully.*' There are many figures of the huts with enclosures, other geometrical ones including a large circle filled with dots, another with square inside it (Pl. XXXIV. 19) and a horned head with two spots between the horns. The whole of the central mass has probably between 1500-1600 figures.

7. *The Small Gully and head of it.*

This is really a part of the central mass but at a lower level. However, it deserves to be mentioned apart, because it is so well marked and because in a small space there are over 500 figures.

We consider this to be one of the most interesting of the Fonta-nalba sub-regions. A deep narrow ravine which joins the cliff of the great gully some way up the central mass cuts it off from the latter. In the ravine itself there are few figures. There are more on the shelf between it and the cliff, but the greater number are to be found where the ravine proper ends, and opens out into a sort of basin with bright yellow rocks and a few steeply inclined fan-shaped surfaces of a rich scarlet colour. Above this basin we climb up rougher rocks without figures and soon reach the higher lake. In this basin, which we call 'The Head of the Little Gully' are figures of all kinds, and many forms of horns not found else-where. (Pl. XXXIV. 20-32). Figs. 20 and 21 are two strange pairs of horned figures. Fig. 22 seems to be a combination of an enclosure with spots and horns. Fig. 26 has branching horns yoked to a plough. Fig. 28 is one of the enclosures with large spots surrounding it. Fig. 27 looks like two united skins with spots between them. On a long narrow surface near the bottom of the region are a number of geometrical forms mostly connected by lines. On a scarlet rock to the left is a horned figure with the upper half of the head not entirely cut out but divided by vertical lines. The figure of two horns pointing in opposite directions and joined to the ends of a rectangle is a form not uncommon in the Meraviglie region but extremely rare in Fontanalba. (Pl. IX. 23). Rare also are the horns like a ram's (Pl. VII. 8). Here are the small group of rectangles with lines and spots (Pl. XVIII. 40) and the horns with a large protuberance between them like the head of an ant (Pl. VIII. 29), and the delicately engraved group of three horns of different sizes (Pl. IX. 14). At the head of the basin under a scarlet fan-shaped surface are four figures of men holding implements. (Pl. XVI. 2). Near to two of them are oxen, if such they be, drawn sideways, as if they had been slain by the mens' axes, but these are certainly cut by different hands and may have no connection with the human figures. This region is soon reached from Lago Verde, and we have spent many a long day there, sometimes having to shelter under a rock from the broiling sun, and at others crouching beneath the northern cliff in storms of pelting rain or snow. On this cliff grow the beautiful *Saxifraga florulenta* and the little *Androsace imbricata*.

8. *The Valley beyond Lago Verde.*

Beyond Lago Verde and the main stream running into it, the valley, fairly level and with much grass, continues for about a kilometre till it is closed by a high rock wall. Under this wall are Dr. Henry's supposed cuneiform characters. There are figures scattered about here and there, most of those in the lower part being on roughish purple rocks. These we did not discover for many years. There are some which it is quite impossible to discern as we pass up in the morning, but which are clear enough on our return in the evening. Fig. 36 of Pl. IX is the first of the engravings which we saw when we first went up to look for them, and it is a curious and unique form. This is on a dark red polished vertical surface a few hundred metres beyond the lake on the right. At the upper part of this valley past some water and marsh land are many smoothish rocks sloping south, but these rather form part of the region next to be described where also the surfaces lie mostly in the same direction. There are over 100 figures in the valley.

9. *The Hillside above the Valley beyond Lago Verde.*

This is bounded by the cliff of the Great Gully, the valley, and the rock wall at the head of it. The rocks are of a grey colour, very different to that of the central mass above the cliff, but there are smooth and coloured surfaces in abundance, which shine brightly when the sun is in the west. (Pl. XXXV. 1). Extremely beautiful is the view from this hillside towards evening, with these shining rocks and the serrated ridge of Monte Bego in the background standing out dark against the sky. The upper limit of this region is not well defined, but we consider it to end at the top of the hill where the character of the rock somewhat changes, and where the great gully, hitherto narrow, opens out into an amphitheatre extending to the foot of the Monte Bego crest. The part richest in engravings is not high above the valley and the brightly coloured rocks are very visible from it. After crossing the

PLATE XXXV.

1. The hillside beyond Lago Verde. 2. 3. Figures on this hillside.

PLATE XXXVI.

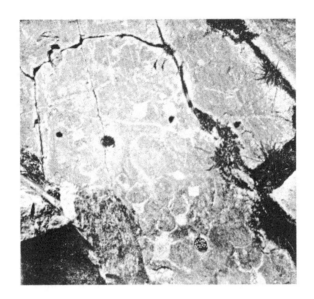

Two portions of the 'Three Hundred' rock. Val Fontanalba.

stream which comes down from the great gully we soon reach the lowest of this series of coloured rocks just above a little rock wall. This has the horns enclosing rectangles (Pl. IX. 1, 2 and XXXV. 2 and Figs. 33, 36, of Plate XXXIV. There is also a large assemblage of figures forming a picture on the village type. A worn large sur- face just above with long lines and large geometrical figures, see- ming to form a large pattern, is the 'Carpet Rock.' On a little shining vertical surface above it is the celebrated scratching of the horse, and a few horns (Pl. VIII. 1). We then come to a splendid surface covered with figures, on one part of which are those of four men brandishing tools or weapons (Pl. XIII. 69). One of them almost seems to be dancing, and we call this the 'Coscritti Rock' as the figures remind us of our young men when called to draw their lots for military service, and who spend the day in shouting and singing. There are also a number of very small figures of men on this rock, some surrounding what looks like a harrow, and others near to what we call huts and enclosures. If these figures were drawn together they may have been intended to represent some sort of pastoral scenes, but on a surface covered over with engravings it is difficult to decide if there be any arrangement of them. On this rock are Pl. XVIII. 32 and XXXIV 34, 35. Some other rocks above this have more or less figures, and then we reach the '300 Rock' with its more than 300 figures covering the greater part of the surface. To this rock we always conduct our visitors who do not wish for a very long excursion. On this are eight figures of ploughs with ploughmen, three harrows, weapons, large rectangles a metre long entirely cut out, enclosures with deeply cut parallel rows of lines in them, and of course, a great variety of the ever-present horns. Some of these are given in Pl. XXXIV. 37-39: III. 11, 19: VII. 3. On the upper part of the rock are the figures of Plate XIII. 51, 52. We cleared away much earth at the foot of this rock, and brought to light many figures long buried. The surfaces which have been long underground are generally quite white, and it is difficult to see the figures. Plate XXXVI. 1, 2 shows the appearance of this remarkable rock. A little below it due south are two or three good rocks, one with four ploughs and men, and the four similar implements or weapons with the straight-edged triangular blades, one, two or three rivets, and their contours and handles engraved not by blows but by scraping. (Pl. XIII. 53-56 also Pls. IX. 37, XIII. 57, XXXVII. 3, 4). Just beyond the *'300 Rock'* we disinterred the large figure Pl. XXXVII. 1. A little farther west is a small upright surface with two knives, a three-horned figure and another extremely curious one. (Pl. VIII. 12 and XXXVII. 2). Farther on and rather lower down we reach the very worn but beautiful *'Tapestry Rock,'* of which we have already spoken in Chapter IV, with the cartouche-like figures forming a very elaborate pattern. From here as far as the gully ending in the rock wall most of the smoother surfaces have figures. We cannot well describe their positions but give copies of many of them. Pl. XXXVII. 7-15 and 17. Those of Pl. XXXVII. 5, 6, are lower down towards the valley. The fig. 5 seems to be that of a man with immensely long legs holding up a small weapon, but it is difficult to say if the two figures are united. The figure XXXVII. 16, is across the upper part of the rock wall. In this region are also Pl. XIII. 60-63, 66, and XX. 10, 11, also the group of 12 beasts (Pl. XLIII. 3).

No part of the Fontanalba region is more difficult to know thoroughly than the steeper parts of the hillside above these. Here are the figures of Plates ·III. 12, VII. 9, IX. 10, 39-41; XIII. 65; and XXXVII. 18-30. The most curious figure among these is the one Pl. XXXVII. 20, XXXV. 3, which looks like the representation of a number of shirts hung out to dry, but which may possibly represent skins. The rock with circles and spade-like forms (Pl. XLIII. 2) was nearly entirely underground. Just at the top of the hill is the figure XVIII. 28, with three others much the same. In the deepest part of the great gully just before it opens out is a rock with two ploughs together and above it one with two figures of men (Pl. XIII. 75) with long snake-like lines, and another with figure much resembling a modern scythe (Pl. XIII. 66). We now descend a little to where there are small ponds. Near these are figures of wide horns very finely and delicately cut. There are about 1700 figures on all this hillside. We now see the broader valley or amphitheatre with the high cliff of the great gully continuing to the north, a steep rocky hillside to the south culminating in a point with a stone cairn, and the scree of the M. Bego crest at the head.

10. *Head of the Great Gully and Amphitheatre.*

On the left bank of the valley are a few figures, but more on the south side including a weapon (Pl. XIII. 68) the long zigzag horns (Pl. XXXVII. 31) towards the cairn a rock with weapons, a spiral, and an eyed beast (Pl. VIII. 51), another with the double-horned figure (Pl. VIII. 11); and close to the cairn the three figures (Pl. XXXVII. 32). More in the central part of the amphitheatre is the three- horned figure (Pl VIII. 14). and high up on the last slopes under the crest some ploughs and other figures and those of Plate XXXVII. 33, 34. In all this higher region the snow lies late and there are many little ponds and many flowers.

11. *The Upper Fontanalba Valley to the Foot of Monte Bego.*

This is the region above the rock wall at the head of the grassy valley beyond Lago Verde. A goat track leads up to it by the south end of the wall, continues west under the scree and then reaches what we may consider to be the continuation of the Fontanalba valley proper, but at a higher level. On the south is a chaos of blocks, and on the north stony or grassy slopes up to the cliffs terminating in the cairn. At the beginning of this upper valley are a good many worn figures chiefly geometrical. There is not much beyond low down worthy of notice except the horizontal horns of Pl. VII. 7, but under the beginning of the cliff a rock with concentric circles (Pl. XVIII. 14) and others which we unearthed, and a little below them the interesting scalariform ones already mentioned, the 'Scale di Paradiso.' Farther a track leads up through the cliffs, passing a rock with spirals and yoked forks and reaches a quantity of large yellow rocks with many good things, and the 'Napoleon Rock' at the end. Some of the figures are given in Pl. XXXVII. 35-45, and XLIII. 5, 6. On the Napoleon rock is the figure Pl. XVIII. 43, and above the cliff those of Pl. XVIII. 41-42 and XIX. Beyond this are more figures, mostly of a rough kind, up to the M. Bego scree and lower down, and on the slopes of the scree are two rocks near together, the 'Monte Bego Village' with its 34 little huts and enclosures etc. Pl. XLIV. 1 and the other Pl. XXXVII. 48. Somewhere near here must be a rock with three horned figures and spots between the horns. These were copied in 1897, but we have never been able to find them again.

The above attempt to describe Val Fontanalba will at least explain to our readers how large a tract of country it is, and how difficult to know thoroughly. We ourselves have each succeeding year been more and more impressed by the strange mystery. However tired we may have been after long days of climbing and descending the rocks, or lying on them in blazing sunshine, or battling with our paper in the wind, we have always been sorry to be obliged to turn our steps homeward before night. Our valley at 1500 m. has seemed hot and stuffy after that purer air above, and after a few days in the valley the solitude of the heights and the fascinating wonders of the rocks have called us up again; and sometimes we have felt that the voices of our prehistoric friends were mingled with the marmot's whistle and the music of the falling streams, and almost expected to find some of them carving their figures and emblems, and be able to ask them who they were, whence they came, and what was the meaning of their work.

PLATE XXXVII.

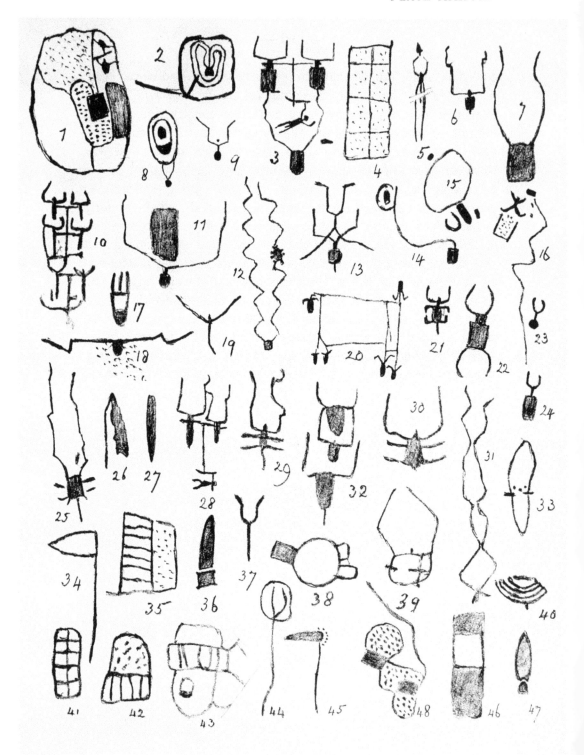

Figures in Val Fontanalba *(continued)*.

CHAPTER VIII.

Guide to the figured rocks in Val Valauretta, Val Valmasca and near Col Sabbione.

There is very little to be said about these regions. The lower part of Val Valauretta consists of pleasant slopes of grass and trees, frequented by a herd of about 400 white cattle. They come every year from Saluzzo to the Margheria del Bosco, which is the name of the cattle shed above the Miniera di Tenda, between it and Val Fontanalba, and they graze not only there, but on the hillsides west of the Val Casterino river and south of the Val Fontanalba one, and also in Valauretta; but they do not go up to the higher part of this valley, which is usually sublet to goat-herds. We have seen a large number of chamois on the snow slopes under the cliffs of Monte Bego very little distant from their near relations the goats. All this upper part of the valley is a wild chaos of rocks. Somewhat above a tiny lake amid the larches, like a miniature Lago Verde, and close under the Monte Bego precipices, may be seen a group of dark purple rocks. It is very difficult to find them when in the valley, but they are most conspicuous from the ridge on the eastern side. Some of these have an almost horizontal surface, others are nearly perpendicular and less weather worn (Pl. 1, 2). There does not seem to have ever been any superficial colouring on most of them. Only one or two are slightly red, but they all have a fairly smooth surface and the upright ones are more highly polished. These have a number of engravings, but while some are perfectly clear, the greater number are scarcely visible. The engravings are rather more deeply cut than is usual, and this was no doubt necessary, if there was never any coating of different colour.

After about another quarter of an hour's scramble further on up the valley and also under the mountain, is another group of similar rocks also engraved and of the same colour and texture. These are more easily found than the first, as they lie near the foot of a steep scree by which the goats descend from the shoulder of Monte Bego, and it was on coming down this ourselves, after an ascent of the mountain, that we lit upon them. Here we have unearthed a good many figures on surfaces covered with grass and the tough roots of Rhododendron bushes, and one which lay hidden under a large and heavy piece of rock.

There seem to be in all between 100-200 engravings. We have copied about 130.

The figures are all cut upon dark purple rocks, layers of which are so conspicuous in the precipices of Monte Bego. On all the smoother yellow rocks in the valley, where we have diligently searched for figures we have found nothing. The figures are for the most part not at all clear, and it is difficult to draw them accurately, and our copies fail to give a good idea of the roughness and irregularities of the originals. All are of the same types. There are no figures of horns or weapons, only rectangles and enclosures, or geometrical forms connected by straight or curved lines. We have found one outline of a rectangle, and one of an oblong with transverse lines. To be sure there are lines cut at right angles which at first sight give the impression of horns, but on closer inspection we were convinced that these are only the beginnings of rectangles. One of the clearest consists of a rectangular figure entirely punched out and with curved enclosure united to a similar figure by a long line, the whole being about 1m. 25c. in length. This is almost the same as a figure in Fontanalba. (Pl. XVIII. 46).

Some of the simple figures have spots in the enclosure and some not. There are also in many places near the figures a great number of spots, apparently of a later date. They do not look very new, as if done by the shepherds of the last few centuries, but as the rock is mostly of the same colour throughout, it is extremely difficult to say whether these dots be really modern or not. We have not seen in this valley any scratchings of names or dates, and have only lately heard after fresh enquiries at Tenda, that some of the figures had been noticed by shepherds, but the famous chamois hunter Signor Palma knew nothing about them, and we think it extremely improbable that they really have been seen by anyone before ourselves.

On the way from the Margheria del Bosco to Val Valauretta, one crosses a ravine which runs down from the ridge of Ciavraireu, and at the bottom of this there are some interesting remains of old enclosures. On the opposite sides of a large and more or less cubical rock two or three metres high, are the remains of two semicircular walls, their ends touching the rock. The somewhat overhanging sides of this have served as a protection, at least from the midday sun, and the pens may have been used to hold a small number of sheep or goats. A few metres off is a rectangular wall, divided by cross walls into three or four partitions. Both of these are exactly like some of the figures engraved on the rocks, and confirm our belief that the primitive huts or shelters for men with adjoining enclosures for beasts were intended to be represented,

Towards the centre of the wide gently sloping land between the upper Lago del Basto and the scree below the Baissa di Valmasca, is a huge erratic block, in the shadow of which the sheep may sometimes be seen reposing in the month of August or later, for there the snow lies a long time and there is very little pasture. This block is a most conspicuous object, such a one as the great purple rock at the Meraviglie, and which might well have seemed a sacred stone fallen from heaven to a little civilized people. Not far from this are a considerable number of rocks with remains of an originally yellow surface, but now extremely splintered. On a few of these are some badly executed and for the most part indistinct figures. One of an ox or horned head is the only thing we have seen of which it was worth while to take a rubbing, but we have not gone over the whole ground, and higher up among the masses of large rocks there may be more. At no period, however, were there any large smooth surfaces inviting the prehistoric sculptors to make their drawings, and the region was farther away from woods and cultivated land than all the others. But we do not feel sure that the shepherds who informed Dr Mader that there were figures in Val Valmasca referred to these. We are surprised if they have noticed these few and inconspicuous ones, and it may well be that there is still some other place which we do not know of. We have spent some time in the Val Valmasca proper, examining in various parts of it the smoother or brighter rock surfaces and also those of gneiss around the Lago Agnel, but we have not found any more signs of man's work.

We have already said how the figures below Col Sabbione may be reached. We only know of about twenty there, most of them very indistinct, but there is one of horned things yoked to a plough, another of a square with two pairs of horns attached, one above and one below, about ten simple horned figures, an oblong and a number of small rectangles. Nearly all of the horns are upright and parallel. We have not explored anywhere else in this neighbourhood.

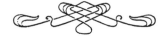

CHAPTER IX.

Guide to the Meraviglie Region.

As we have only spent 33 days in the Meraviglie region, and have not been able to explore some parts of it even twice, we do not know exactly where some of the principal figures are to be found again, and no doubt there are many more which we have not seen. There are probably more on the purple rocks round about the Laghi Lunghi and other lakes, on which kind of rocks it is by no means easy to find them. Probably many on the steep slopes of Monte Bego have escaped us. As far as we can see, looking at these slopes from the opposite side of the valley, there are no more glacier-polished and coloured surfaces higher up than where we have been, but we are not sure, and there also, as lower down, figures may have been engraved on other kinds of surfaces. We have only been twice on this steeper part, and many of the figures have not been found a second time. We also know that there are many more not copied above the lower part of the right bank of the Vallone, for when this last summer we were descending the corner between the Vallone and the Arpeto valley we saw several, but were unable to stop, as a violent storm of rain and hail drove us away, and anyhow we should have been obliged to leave on account of the lateness of the hour. We can, however, describe this region of the Meraviglie better than that of Fontanalba. There are no Ciappe so puzzling as the great central mass in this latter.

1. *The Left Bank of the Laghi Lunghi.*

On reaching the Val d'Inferno the path crosses to the left bank of the river. All about here are smoothish purple or reddish surfaces. About 50 m. beyond the bridge, on a vertical rock near the path, is cut in large letters the name *Bolla*. Two years ago this name attracted the soldiers to cut theirs also there. It is a pity, as there are 13 of the prehistoric figures on the rock, and they have been nearly destroyed. On other rocks of the same kind nearer M. Bego and a goatshed, and between there and a rock-shelter where the soldiers usually encamp, and where we have always pitched our tent, are a good many figures, but nearly all horns of much the same shape. We know of about 50 in all. There do not seem to be others till towards the end of the upper lake, where, some way above it and above a goat track leading to the Vallone, are a quantity of dark rocks without any polished or coloured surface, and in great confusion. Leaving the track and mounting up among them we come to several just below a col from which one descends to the little meadow at the bottom of the Vallone. Here are between 40 and 50 figures, a plough, a few horns, and the rest mostly geometrical ones, some of strange forms unlike anything in Val Fontanalba. They are roughly but deeply cut, for as there was no thin coloured coating to cut away, it was probably necessary to cut more deeply to make the engravings stand out clearly (Pl. XXII. 1-8).

2. *The Left Bank of the Vallone.*

After turning the corner to ascend the Vallone we come to a flat meadow. East of this among the rocks lying about everywhere, and on the north side of it under the cliffs facing us, are many figures. There are some especially good ones just under the highest cliff; a cross with branching arms, a weapon with ornamented blade etc. (Pl. XI. 12, 17; XXII. 14; XXXVIII. 1, 4, 19, 20). A short ascent west of the cliff leads to a more or less level region above the river, at the end of which one may descend into the Vallone, but north and east are cliffs which prevent further progress along this part of the M. Bego slopes. This small region is interesting from the number of good figures. Here are the weapons with fringed handles, the cross with three spots at the end of each arm, several strange things, and what may probably be some intentional groups (Pl. XI. 1, 2, 9, 10; XXII. 12; XXXVIII. 2, 3, 5-18). There are in all about 200 figures. Near the path by the river below are a few, and where there is a narrow passage between the rocks are about 25 figures, including many weapons, cut on the rock wall. Here Pietro Palma, the well-known shepherd and chamois hunter, has left his handiwork, as he has done in so many other places. He is generally known by his nickname 'Pelle,' that is 'Skin,' and in the prehistoric days would probably have cut a skin on the rocks to signify the same. A little farther on above the path are three figures, one rather like a face, (Plate XXXVIII. 21, 22). We then reach the lower Meraviglie lake.

3. *Left Bank of the Lower Lago delle Meraviglie*:

At the beginning of the lake a steep yellow rock runs down into the water, and must be crossed on a little ledge, one of the grooves formed by ice and water. On the upper part of this are about 80 figures, chiefly horns, but there are two or three figures nearly worn away, of a curious kind. Farther on and a little higher is another smoother surface with one large weapon, another with horns cut across it, several geometrical figures, and two others which much resemble some near the Lago del Carbone, all of them being forms peculiar to the Meraviglie. (Pl. XXXVIII. 23-25). There are here 50 figures. Between the last two rocks, but considerably higher, is a similar smooth rock with about 50 figures, including one like the strange ones just mentioned, and also some horizontal horns nearly 2½ metres long, and close to the point of the right hand one or touching it, is the figure of a man with club-shaped feet, and holding an implement over his head in the act of striking. This is the second largest human figure anywhere (Pl. XXXVIII. 26, 27; XLIII. 7). We then go along past the lake, and come to a few high smooth rocks, on the flat top of one of which are more than 100 figures. We call this the *'Bird Rock'* on account of a figure not unlike a bird flying, and there are three others much the same, also many geometrical or net figures, 14 weapons or implements of various shapes, six of them close together, many fork-like horns, and one like a pitchfork with handle nearly a metre long. (XXXVIII. 28-32; VII. 46). The other rocks near have a few figures. Beyond these a sort of grassy avenue leads up towards Monte Bego. On the right or south side are two much decorated surfaces, the lower with 12, the upper with more than

70 figures. (XXXVIII. 33-35). One seems to be a man pulling a harrow or net, another a man holding up a pitchfork, that is if the two parts are united. There is also the figure of an axe, one of two concentric circles with spot in the centre, a broken plough, some knives, and a head like that of an ox with little lines on the top between the horns like a fringe. On the left side of the avenue is a rock which we have in part unearthed, with one of the most complicated of the special kind of Meraviglie geometrical figures, three quarters of a metre long. Left of this, and out of sight from the avenue, are some very worn rocks with about 40 figures. At the end of the avenue is the most wonderful rock of all, where we have copied nearly 450 figures, but we cannot be sure that we have copied all of them. It is a pity that noone except our friends to whom we explained its position, seems to have seen it, for to see this one rock alone is well worth a long journey It is much finer than the rocks in the 'défilé,' of which we shall speak later, and than the '300 rock' in Val Fontanalba. We call it the 'Altar Rock,' for if in the whole region there was one spot more sacred or more frequented than another, this is surely it. It is a large convex surface, very smooth and yellow on the south side, grey and roughish on the north. (Pl. XXXIX.). On the top of it is an immense boulder of purple anagenite, strangely contrasting with the rock on which it stands. It rests on a very small base, and looks almost like a rocking stone. There is nothing else at all like this, and nowhere else is the view all around more magni-ficent. The great cliffs of Monte Bego are on one side, the peak and slaty pinnacles of Gran Capelet on the other, with the fine summit of the Rocca delle Meraviglie. All around in the valley is a chaos of blocks heaped one upon the other. But alas! not every-one can respect and admire this astonishing surface, and a person to whom we pointed this out has cut on the yellow side two white initials in the middle of the figures, so that now there is this ugly scar defacing what before had never been spoiled through all the centuries, and in shade and sunshine alike it stands out crying shame. A loose piece of rock stands near the top, and ought to be removed for a museum, although the 11 figures on it are not at all good ones; but it must be of great weight and we do not know

PLATE XXXVIII.

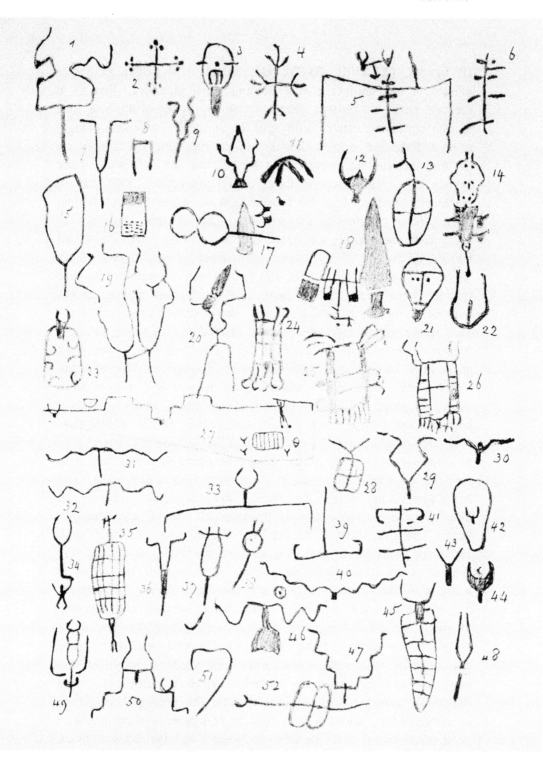

Figures in the Meraviglie region.

how it could be carried down to the valley. Probably a mule cannot reach the lake except by the way of Val Valmasca. On the south side of the Altar Rock are about 130 figures with many forms not found elsewhere, and a large number of most irregular and intricate net forms, and about 12 weapons and implements. On the north side are nearly 90 figures of weapons, over 200 horned figures and much besides; but the figures are so close to one another and even interlacing, that it is extremely difficult to copy them, and though we have spent many days 'there we do not feel sure that we have finished. It is only in the early morning and towards evening that many of them can be clearly seen (Pl. XI. 24, 29, 31-33, 40; XXII. 20-26; XXIII. 4; XXXVIII. 36-46; XLII. 38). One of the spear-heads is over 80 c. long. The curious figure XI. 29, which we have published twice before, but the first time not quite correctly, as we had not observed the spots which evidently form part of the drawing, may perhaps represent, according to Prof. Issel, some kind of ritual sickle. The three interlacing horns (Pl. XLII. 38) seem to be the only figures forming a group.

4. *The steep sides of Monte Bego.*

There are two distinct parts easy to find. One is that which is directly above the higher part of the Vallone and lake, where many rows of steep rounded glaciated rocks may be seen from below, and the other, which does not look at all promising, is above the little amphitheatre beyond the Altar Rock. From the foot of this latter, one can easily ascend to the crest north of the summit of M. Bego, and so cross over into Val Fontanalba. We have sometimes gone home that way, but after a long day's work the ascent is rather fatiguing, and we generally return by the Miniera. At various places on this route are figures, but we have only found about 40 in all. Two of them are shown in Plate XI. 48, 49. On the other part which has many interesting forms there are some 240 figures or more. (Pl. XI. 55, 57; XXXVIII. 47-52; XLI. 1, 2). One rock has a large number of small forks, (Pl. XLII. 36). On another we descried on our last visit some extremely diminutive horns. We thought before that the smallest pair were in Val Fontanalba, of which the figure Pl. XLIII. 8 is an exact copy; but

one on this rock only measures 1 ¹/₂ c. × 1c., and is most beautifully cut out by a multitude of tiny holes. What a difference in
the dimensions of this to the pair of horns on the opposite side
of the Vallone which measure 269 c. × 273 c. There are many geometrical figures also here and one pair of horns, the head of which
has only the contour drawn.

5. *The valley beyond the lower lake, and near its right bank.*

There are only a very few figures a long way up the valley
where is a pond formed by the melting snow, but a little beyond
the lake on the right bank of the stream is a rock just by the
water with 10 figures, some of which were published by M. Rivière
and others, and there are a few others near it. At the extreme
lower end of the lake are some which we were able to copy after
removing a large block partly covering them. It was while I was
near this one day in 1909 that my companion who had gone on
ahead returned in a great state of excitement shouting out " I have
found the Chief of the Tribes." He had discovered the rock which
we have already mentioned in Chapter IV. (Pl. XVII). This was
indeed a reward after a trying day, for it had rained at intervals,
and we had lost much time in being obliged to shelter ourselves
and more precious paper under protecting rocks till the weather
cleared again and the rocks were dry. The figure of the man
measures 50 c. × 28 c.

6. *The Hillside between the Lower and Upper Lakes.*

There are over 150 figures between the two lakes. There is
one of a dagger with very broad hilt, and two others, one of
them showing three rivets and another with handle in two parts
divided from the blade. (Pl. XI. 64 - 66). A square, symmetrically divided vertically and horizontally, is well cut, and there are
two horned figures, which M. Clugnet copied, with spots between
the horns and also strange projections. These are together near
the upper lake. (Pl. XLI. 5-10). The masses of schist fallen from
the Rocca delle Meraviglie are heaped one upon the other here,
and the engraving on one smooth surface we have been unable to
copy as it was impossible for us to remove a block upon it. Round

and beyond this lake there seem to be no more figures. There are
some yellowish rocks towards the third and highest lake, which
we have not ourselves examined, but friends who have been there
on purpose assure us that there is nothing.

7. *The Rock Waves.*

From somewhat below the upper lake we can cross the scree
horizontally under the Rocca delle Meraviglie, and reach a beautiful region of coloured rocks which are very conspicuous from the
Laghi Lunghi. One can come down to these rocks from the crest
of the hill above them or find an approach on their south side;
but the region lies at the top of a cliff above the Vallone, and
this cliff cannot be climbed, at least by people who are not devoted to climbing. We usually take the path up the right bank of
the Vallone, and when above the lower lake mount a little as if
going on to the upper lake, and then double back. This is the
best way of reaching the 'Rock Waves,' as we enter the region
nearer the bottom of it, and can then gradually mount, wave after
wave, looking at the figures which are mostly sloping towards the
valley. These waves or banks of rock are perhaps the smoothest
and brightest in the whole region. They are exceedingly beautiful.
They are more or less in parallel rows and the figures upon them
are for the most part well cut and very clear. We have counted
over 400 figures on them, but there is room for tens of thousands.
Most of these rocks do not seem to have changed at all since the
figures were engraved, or indeed since the ice left them. They
must be well protected by snow the greater part of the year and
the rain of summer storms rapidly runs off them. One can only
regret that there are not more figures, as it is a delight to walk
gradually up backwards and forwards among these terraces without
any fatigue, enchanted by the rich colours of the rocks, the variety
of the engravings and the glorious view. On reaching this region
at the northern end, the first long rounded wave, but in this case
much worn, is the one with the coat of arms of Humberto Del
Agarena and quantities of modern inscriptions. Farther on, much
on the same level, is a wave with a wheel-like figure and what
may perhaps be that of a man apparently attached to it. (Pl. XXII.

108

38). On another near are the figure with the 'Alphabetical' forms (Pl. XXIII. 1-2) and other large ones of somewhat similar character (Pl. XXII. 33; XXIII. 2, 3). All the figures given in our Plates VII. 45; IX. 17, 20, 21, 24; XII. 1-6, 8, 9, 16-18; XXII. 33-40; XXIII 1-3, 21; XLI. 11-18, 40, 41; XLII. 33-35, are here. There are a good many plough figures of the type of Pl. III. 16. We must call attention to a few of these figures, to the long horizontal horns facing each other (Pl. IX. 17); to the figure with horns joined at the top and with two others inside the hoop (Pl. XLI. 15); to the strange form (Pl. XLI. 17). which was figured by Moggridge but upside down; to the figure (Pl. XLII. 33) measuring 303 c. $\times$ 56 c.; to the largest horns known of which we have spoken (Pl. XLII. 35), and to two others also published by Moggridge but inaccurately or only partially drawn. He speaks of one, the figure (Pl. XLII. 34) as " the counterpart of an engraving in an old book in the great library of Turin where it is called Idol Sarde." It appears to be a group of horns of various shapes and sizes, and when compared with other groups not much more remarkable. The other could not have been faithfully copied because a large part of it was underground. (Pl. XL. 2 and Pl. XLI. 16). This is a kind of horned figure with some horizontal lines, and a vertical one down part of its length. The tops of the horns are capped by unmistakeable figures of a hand with the five fingers very clearly cut, and just touching each hand is a triangular blade pointing in a horizontal direction. For some years we were unable to suggest any sort of interpretation of this curious design. Then one day when we saw it for the third or fourth time we noticed that there were two round holes, one on either side of the top of the vertical line, and we were convinced that the figure was intended to represent a human face with eyes, nose, and mouth fairly well indicated. It suggests a mask or some frightful face to terrify others, and appears the more alarming on account of the uplifted hands on either side of the head grasping daggers. In 1908 we mentioned this additional discovery, but the matter did not end then, for this last summer we have made another discovery. Wishing to photograph the figure again, as the light was exceptionally good, and the disinterred part of the figure seemed much clearer than usual, we

PLATE XXXIX.

1. The north side of 'Altar Rock.'

2. The south side.

PLATE XL.

1. Figures on the south side of 'Altar Rock.'

2. Figures on the 'Rock Waves.'

washed the rock and scraped away the lichen in the grooves of the engraving, and then found that the supposed horizontal line at the bottom is not a line, but composed of seven spots in a row. These clearly represent teeth in the mouth, and the likeness to a human face is still more complete. Our Plate XLI. 16 then, drawn before this discovery, is no more completely accurate than the first one, and our readers must substitute seven spots for the straight line as in the Pl. XL. 2. This little story shows how difficult it is to copy figures really correctly, and warns us that many others may not have been accurately copied. At the crest of the hill above the Rock Waves is a vertical surface, much disfigured by a very new but happily unfinished modern engraving, but it has 30 prehistoric figures including some branching horns, (Pl. VII. 5), two knives, (Pl. XII. 17, 18) one with hole in the blade and the other with ornamented handle, and three pairs of horns facing each other.

8. The Défilé.'

This is the narrow passage under the cliffs below the Rock Waves, so called by M. Rivière. It is the upper part of the foot-path on the right bank of the Vallone, for this path which mounts for some time near the stream is arrested some little way above the meadow where M. Rivière pitched his tent by rocks coming down to the water, and one has to mount under the cliffs by a sort of staircase, at the top of which the track passes between the cliff and two long glaciated figured surfaces. These two surfaces have nearly 300 engravings. On the upper one is a figure like a wooden club (Pl. XII. 20), two figures of implements with horns cut across them (Pl. XLII. 31, 32) many weapons, an immense number of small horns, the figures of Pl. XLI. 19-21, and the complicated figure of seven horns of which two seem to be part of a plough with three others in the same horizontal line and two more above. (Pl. XLII. 37). On the lower surface is the elaborate geometrical figure (Pl. XXIII. 6), a large group of them (Pl. XXIII. 25), horns with the later addition of a cross between them and others (Pl. XLI. 22, 23). Below these on a ledge of the cliff, not visible from the path, and above it, is a surface with a number

of geometrical figures, and by the path two others where M. Rivière copied much. One is certainly the figure of a man, another
of branching horns (Pl. VII. 6), another published by Rivière resem-
bles a bag or basket with handle (Pl. XLI. 24, 25), and also the
very large figure (Pl. XXIII. 11) measuring 83 c. × 185 c. and perhaps still longer. The part of it like a wheel with a line attached
is in M. Rivière's Plate, and looks like the drawing of a country
cart. Prof. Issel has alluded to this figure, but as may be seen it
is only a very small piece of an immense figure. It is quite certain
that the cart portion is not detached from the rest, but we do not
wonder if the whole of this figure was not noticed and only the
more attractive part of it selected to be copied, for here more than
anywhere the figures are becoming very much worn, not from the
weather but from the nailed boots of visitors; for, as we have said,
this is the place where everybody goes, and these are figures
which everybody sees. Anyone wishing to visit the 'Wonders' is
told to follow the path on the right bank of the Vallone, and then
he cannot fail to come to these rocks and to walk about on them.

9. *The right bank of the Vallone below the 'Défilé.'*

Below the staircase we descend to the grassy amphitheatre,
Rivière's meadow, in which are a few figures (Pl. XXIII. 14) as
also on the way down to it, but they are abundant on the hillside
above, and are to be found more or less on all the coloured rocks
with smooth surfaces, and on some few others also. It is not possible to describe the position of many of these, and we shall not
attempt it but only mention a few Some way directly above the
meadow is a very clean smooth horizontal surface where M. Rivière
copied much, and which has 93 figures. An interesting one is Pl.
XXIII. 13, one of the numerous geometrical figures. Close to it is
a weapon, perhaps a halberd with three rivets, the handle ending
in horns with a small pair of horns between them. (Pl. XXIV. 2).
The figures of Pl. XLI. 26-27; XXIII. 18, 22, are on this rock.
Close by is another with about 25 figures including XXIII. 8-10.
The figures XXIII. 19, 23; XLI. 28-39, 42, 43, 45, 46, 48-51, are
probably all on this hillside nearest the Laghi Lunghi, but one or
two may be elsewhere. The eight-rayed star, in Plate XLI, is near

PLATE XLI.

Figures in the Meraviglie region *(continued)*.

PLATE XLII.

Figures in the Meraviglie region *(continued)*.

the lake. We do not know this part at all well nor the corner of the hill and slopes towards Val Arpeto.

10. *Val della Rocca.*

We shall never forget the day when first we climbed to the crest above the Rock Waves. It was late in the afternoon, and after a very long day's work it was time to return to our camp. We had no idea of the surprise which awaited us, for on the other side of the crest westward was a short but deepish valley running up to the foot of the Rocca delle Meraviglie, and it seemed to be filled with smooth yellow rocks. Could there be also engravings there? We could not resist the temptation to descend, and on the very first bright surface we reached were many figures. Since then we have spent many days there, and have found about 450 figures. One surface in the middle of the valley is covered with 80 of them. Another quite level with the soil, which we partly unearthed, has only large circles or similar forms. (Pl. VII. 11; XII. 48; XLI. 53-55; XLII. 1-12). As will be seen there are many very remarkable forms of horned figures, and some to which we can give no interpretation. Perhaps they were the private marks of those who cut them, perhaps merely their artistic fancies, but we have found in regions far apart the repetition of some strange figure, which gives the idea that the same sculptor has engraved his own particular sign more than once.

11. *The Arpeto Region.*

Beyond the western boundary of this valley is one more valley or depression extending to the highest crest overlooking the Gordolasca valley, and here are about 220 figures. Some of the best are towards the top of the hillside above the Arpeto valley. Here is one of the best figures of horns with spots or thick lines between and below them, a figure of yoked animals with very long plough pole and, as far as we know, the only one in the Meraviglie region, where the side appendages which we call the legs are shown; also a weapon with horns on the point (Pl. III. 18; IX. 3; XLII. 13-19). There is also the scythe, or whatever it be, with four spots (Pl. XII. 64), and almost in the valley an implement with long handle over a metre in length. The yellow rocks extend almost to the Arpeto crest but there are no figures on the higher ones.

12. *The Arpeto Valley.*

Besides the figures near the head of the valley just mentioned, and those on the northern slopes, there are a considerable number on rocks at the lower part of the valley, chiefly on the dark red or purple rocks. Very probably there are more here which we have not seen. One deserves special mention. There is a pond in the valley not far from the head of the upper of the Laghi Lunghi. Beyond this pond, on the side of the conspicuous peak dividing the Arpeto and Trem valleys, are a quantity of large blocks mostly fallen from the mountain. Among these we have lately found a dark purple one, partly covered by other rocks, on which are 24 figures, including one of two large yoked horned figures and very small ploughshare. Though this rock must have been engraved before the fall of the other rocks, it is a most extraordinary place to have cut anything, for the barren mountain side can never have been attractive to man or beast. (Pl. XLII. 27-30). The question why figures were cut at all in such strange places as this, and on rocks which did not offer any attractive smooth and brilliantly coloured surface, is a very puzzling one. Close by were the Rock Waves, the most attractive of all for engravings. It seems that some of the sculptors purposely did their work where it would be most concealed, and where only they themselves, if they ever returned again, would be able to find it.

13. *The Right Bank of the Laghi Lunghi.*

The path from the Miniera, after crossing the lower end of the lower of the two Laghi Lunghi by a causeway of stones, mounts gradually, leaving the lake some way below. Before reaching the mountain dividing the Arpeto and Trem valleys, if we leave the path and ascend a little to the left, we see another small lake, Lago Forcato. Between the path and this lake, and on several rocks just above it, all of the purple colour, are figures. We have found between 80 and 90. Those close to the lake were

PLATE XLIII.

1-6. Figures in Val Fontanalba. - 7. By Lago delle Meraviglie.
8. The smallest horned figure in Val Fontanalba.

only discovered in 1911, and some of them are very strange forms and have a certain resemblance to the ones we have mentioned near the Meraviglie lake. (Pl. XLII. 20-23). We can suggest no explanation of these figures.

14. *The Regions of Lago Carbone and Laghi del Trem.*

From Lago Forcato we can climb up among some of the large masses of 'roches moutonnées' to the high land above the Lago Carbone. In this region are about ten surfaces, all purple ones, with figures, and some of them extremely good ones. There are two on the same rock, of the last-mentioned curious type. (Pl. XLII. 25, 26). Another has figures of twelve weapons of different forms, another eight and one horned one (Pl. XII. 40-42). We can then descend to the two Laghi del Trem. By the left bank of the upper one are three figured rocks (Pl. XLII. 24), and we think that we once saw more nearer to Cima del Diavolo. We could not find any on our last visit, but it was a very cursory one as we were driven away by a violent storm of hail. This region then is not yet fully explored, and perhaps we may say the same of all the others. We have certainly largely extended the knowledge of the whole Meraviglie region, and the 'Wonders' near the Laghi delle Meraviglie, of which Gioffredo wrote and which all visitors hitherto have believed to be only there, are but a part of the whole number of them.

BIBLIOGRAPHY

P. GIOFFREDO. *Storia delle Alpi Marittime, 1650* Vol. I. p. 67, published in Torino, 1824.

F. C. FODÉRÉ. *Voyage aux Alpes Maritimes.* Paris, 1821.

E. RECLUS. *Les Villes d'hiver de la Mediterranée et les Alpes Maritimes.* p. 379.

M. MOGGRIDGE. *The Meraviglie. Proceedings of the International Congress of Prehistoric Anthropology and Archæology.* London, 1868.

HENRY. *Une excursion aux Lacs des Merveilles etc. Annales de la Société des Lettres etc. des Alpes Maritimes.* Tome IV. Nice, 1877.

L. CLUGNET. *Sculptures Préhistoriques situées sur les bords des Lacs des Merveilles. Materiaux pour l'Histoire Primitive et Naturelle de l'homme.* Vol. XII. pp. 379-387. Toulouse, 1877.

E. BLANC. *Études sur les Sculptures Préhistoriques du Val d'Enfer.* Cannes, 1878.

E. RIVIÈRE. *Gravures sur roches des Lacs des Merveilles au Val d'Enfer. Association Française pour l'avancement des sciences.* Paris, 1878.

S. NAVELLO. *Impressioni sulle iscrizioni simboliche preistoriche dei Laghi delle Meraviglie. Bollettino del Club Alpino Italiano.* Torino, 1884.

A. F. PRATO. *Sulle iscrizioni simboliche del Lago delle Meraviglie. Rivista Alpina Italiana.* Torino, 1884.

E. D'ALBERTIS. *Crociera del "Corsaro" alle Isole Canarie.* pp. 69, 70. Milano, 1884.

E. CELESIA. *I Laghi delle Meraviglie in Val d'Inferno.* Genova, 1885.

»　　» *Bollettino Ufficiale del Ministero della Pubblica Istruzione.* Vol. XII. Roma, 1886.

C. BICKNELL. *Le figure incise sulle rocce di Val Fontanalba. Atti della Società Ligustica di Scienze Naturali.* Anno VIII. Fasc. IV. Genova, 1897.

C. BICKNELL.   *Osservazioni ulteriori sulle incisioni rupestri in Val Fontanalba. Atti etc. Anno X. Fasc. I. Genova, 1889.*

LISSAUER.   *Anthropologischer Bericht über seine letzte. Reise in Süd-Frankreich und Italien. Verhandl. der Berliner Anthrop. Gesellschaft. Sitzung 21 Juli, 1900. Berlin.*

F. MADER.   *Le rupi scolpite dei Laghi delle Meraviglie e di Val Fontanalba. Rivista del Club Alpino Italiano. Vol. XX. Marzo, 1901.*

A. ISSEL.   *Le Rupi scolpite nelle alte valli delle Alpi Marittime. Boll. di Paletnologia Italiana. Anno XXVII. N. 10-12. Parma, 1901.*

C. BICKNELL.   *The Prehistoric Rock Engravings in the Italian Maritime Alps. Bordighera, 1902.*

»   »   *Further Explorations etc. Bordighera, 1903.*

»   »   *Incisioni rupestri nuovamente osservate etc. Atti della Società Ligustica etc. Vol. XVII. 1906, Genova.*

A. ISSEL.   *Liguria Preistorica. pp. 485-559. Genova, 1908.*

C. BICKNELL.   *Nuovo contributo alla cognizione delle incisioni rupestri etc. Atti della Soc. Ligustica etc. Vol. XIX. 1908, Genova.*

»   »   *La Prahistoriaj Gravurajôoj sur rokoj en la Italaj Maralpoj. Internacia Scienca Revuo. Genève, 1909.*

A. STIEGELMANN.   *Les Petroglyphes des Alpes Maritimes. La Revue Préhistorique. Juillet, 1909. Paris.*

»   »   *Les Petroglyphes des Alpes Maritimes. Revue de l'École d'Anthropologie. Mars, 1910.*

P. RAYMOND.   *Une Visite aux Roches gravées de Fontanalba. La Revue Préhistorique. Octobre, 1910. Paris.*

DIARD.   *Dessins préhistoriques sur roches des Alpes Maritimes. Société d'histoire naturelle d'Autun. 1911, Autun.*

A. STIEGELMANN.   *Les Petroglyphes des Alpes Maritimes. La Revue Préhistorique. Octobre, 1910. Paris.*

»   »   *Nouvelles découvertes de roches gravées dans les Alpes Maritimes Italiennes. La Revue Préhistorique. Avril, 1911. Paris.*

Allusions to the rock figures may also be found in the following books:

The Mediterranean Race. Prof. SERGI, p. 394. Rome, 1901. *Along the Rivieras of France and Italy.* GORDON HOME, pp. 123-126. London, 1908. *The Stone and Bronze Ages in Italy.* T. E. PEET, pp. 392-394. Oxford 1909. *The Dawn of Mediterranean Civilization.* A. MOSSO, pp. 20-22. London, 1910.

The actual dimensions in centimetres of the figures on the rocks.

PLOUGHS etc.

PLATE III.

Ploughs with men.

1. 38 × 33 Fontanalba.
2. 27 ¹/₂ × 36 ¹/₂ »
3. 29 × 28 »
4. 12 × 15 »
5. 27 × 18 ¹/₂ »
6. 31 × 29 ¹/₂ »
7. 56 × 45 ¹/₂ »
8. 50 × 25 »
9. 45 × 23 »
10. 36 × 30 »
11. 44 × 28 »
12. 29 × 19 ¹/₂ »

Ploughs without men

13. 15 × 27 »
14. 35 × 41 »
15. 122 × 66 »
16. 34 × 35 ¹/₂ Meraviglie
17. 23 × 18 »
18. 45 × 19 »

Harrows.

19. 19 × 19 Fontanalba.
20. 20 × 20 »
21. 19 × 20 ¹/₂ »

Horned figures yoked.

22. 16 × 20 Fontanalba.
23. 39 × 27 »
24. 25 × 29 ¹/₂ »
25. 35 ¹/₂ × 36 »
26. 14 ¹/₂ × 20 »
27. 17 ¹/₂ × 28 ¹/₂ »
29. 23 × 13 ¹/₂ Meraviglie
29. 10 × 32 ¹/₂ »

PLATE IV.

Plough with oxen and three men
in V. Fontanalba. 36 × 30.

PLATE V.

Napoleon Rock. Plough with
man. 42 × 39.

PLATE VI.

1. Plough without man in the
Arpeto region. 28 × 24 ¹/₂.

2. Oxen with harrow. Val Fontanalba. 19 × 19.

HORNED FIGURES.

PLATE VII.

Branching horns.
1. 21½ × 16   Fontanalba.
2. 30   × 25   »
3. 12   × 17½   »
4. 57   × 18   »
5. 26   × 22   Meraviglie.
6. 16½ × 33½   »

Horizontal horns.
7. 20   × 68   Fontanalba.
8. 10   × 15   »
9. 30   × 142   »
10. 22½ × 50   »
11. 9 ½ × 38   Meraviglie.

Upright horns.
12. 43½ × 18   Fontanalba.
13. 56   × 19   »
14. 48½ × 15   »
15. 45½ × 22½   »
16. 22½ × 13½   »
17. 21   × 17   Meraviglie.
18. 25½ × 9   Fontanalba.
19. 27½ × 13½ Meraviglie

Zigzag and waving horns.
20. 57   × 24   Fontanalba.
21. 82   × 42½   »
22. 30   × 28½   »
23. 84   × 40   »
24. 40   × 14½   »
25. 79   × 75   »

Horns of common shapes.
26. 34   × 25   Fontanalba.
27. 12   × 11   »
28. 16½ × 20   »
29. 28   × 23   »
30. 34   × 27   »
31. 22   × 31   »
32. 14   × 26   »
33. 42   × 23   »

Fork-like horns.
34. 15   × 14   »
35. 24   × 16½   »
36. 20   × 12   »
37. 13   × 8   »
38. 14   × 12   Meraviglie.
39. 20   × 16   »
40. 12½ × 8   »
41. 21   × 10   »
42. 17   × 11   »
43. 14   × 11   »
44. 38   × 20   »

Long forks.
45. 83   × 18   »
46. 93   × 17   »

Horns nearly joined.
47. 19   × 18   Fontanalba.
47ᵃ 16   × 17   »
48. 23   × 14   »

Horns joined.
49. 24   × 13   »
50. 45½ × 15   »
51. 25   × 15   »

Horns with loops.
52. 27   × 19   »

HORNED FIGURES.

PLATE VIII.

Horns with crossbar.	1. $18^{1}/_{2} \times 8$	Fontanalba
	1ª 13 $\times 9$	»
	2. $20^{1}/_{2} \times 16$	»
	3. 31 $\times 16$	»
	4. 18 $\times 11$	Meraviglie
	5. 19 $\times 15^{1}/_{2}$	»
Double horns.	6. 20 $\times 18$	Fontanalba
	7. $18^{1}/_{2} \times 19$	»
	8. 8 $\times 9^{1}/_{2}$	»
	9. 15 $\times 3$	»
	10. 17 $\times 22$	»
	11. 18 $\times 11$	»
Three horns.	12. 17 $\times 12$	»
	13. 41 $\times 25$	»
	14. 55 $\times 29$	»
	15. 27 $\times 21^{1}/_{2}$	»
	16. 24 $\times 29^{1}/_{2}$	»
	17. $12^{1}/_{2} \times 8$	»
Horns with neck.	18. 25 $\times 13$	»
	19. 33 $\times 33$	»
With square round oblong or triangular head.	20. 14 $\times 12$	»
	21. $12^{1}/_{2} \times 8$	»
	22. 12 $\times 8$	»
	23. 12 $\times 11$	»
	24. 16 $\times 22$	»
	25. 12 $\times 19$	»
With weapon-like head.	26. 31 $\times 24$	»

With appendage to head.	27. 16 $\times 15^{1}/_{2}$	Fontanalba
	28. 16 $\times 19$	»
	29. 38 $\times 21$	»
	30. 39 $\times 48$	»
	31. 13 $\times 10$	»
With ears.	32. 33 $\times 24$	»
	33. 10 $\times 11$	»
With ears and tail.	34. 33 $\times 22$	»
	35. 36 $\times 20$	»
	36. 30 $\times 19$	»
With ears.	37. 23 $\times 12$	»
With legs.	38. $38^{1}/_{2} \times 17$	»
	39. 27 $\times 11$	»
	40. 21 $\times 20$	»
	41. 31 $\times 12$	»
	42. 30 $\times 17$	»
With legs.	43. 15 $\times 10^{1}/_{2}$	»
	44. 18 $\times 11$	»
	45. 22 $\times 11$	»
With ears legs and tail.	46. 21 $\times 4^{1}/_{2}$	»
With tail and appendage.	47. 26 $\times 11$	»
	48. 26 $\times 20$	»
	49. 16 $\times 8$	»
With eyes.	50. 37 $\times 19$	»
	51. 26 $\times 14$	»

PLATE IX.

Horns with rectangles or spots

1. $10\,^1/_2 \times 9\,^1/_2$ Fontanalba
2. 12 $\times 10$ »
3. 34 $\times 31$ Meraviglie
4. 15 $\times 13\,^1/_2$ »
5. 16 $\times 8\,^1/_2$ Fontanalba

Horned figures two together.

6. 16 $\times 20$ »
7. 23 $\times 10$ »
8. $11\,^1/_2 \times 7$ »
9. 21 $\times 18$ »
10. 58 $\times 25$ »
11. 22 $\times 12$ »

Horned figures three together.

12. 26 $\times 20$ »
13. 26 $\times 26$ »
14. $14\,^1/_2 \times 10$ »
15. $39\,^1/_2 \times 23$ »
16. 69 $\times 45$ »

Two horned figures facing.

17. $18\,^1/_2 \times 36\,^1/_2$ Meraviglie
18. 27 $\times 11\,^1/_2$ »
19. 27 $\times 14\,^1/_2$ »
20. 31 $\times 15\,^1/_2$ »
21. 26 $\times 9$ »
22. $29\,^1/_2 \times 20$ »

Horns in opposite directions.

23. 19 $\times 6\,^1/_2$ Fontanalba
24. 18 $\times 15\,^1/_2$ Meraviglie
25. 30 $\times 9\,^1/_2$ Fontanalba

Various curious figures of horns.

26. 39 $\times 10$ Fontanalba.
27. 46 $\times 26$ »
28. 58 $\times 48$ »
29. $30\,^1/_2 \times 19$ »
30. $19\,^1/_2 \times 10\,^1/_2$ »
31. $31\,^1/_2 \times 28$ »
32. 9 $^1/_2 \times 14\,^1/_2$ »
33. 50 $\times 27$ »
34. $29\,^1/_2 \times 20$ »
35. 35 $\times 9$ »
36. 17 $\times 17$ »
37. 22 $\times 25$ »
38. $36\,^1/_2 \times 46$ »
39. $17\,^1/_2 \times 7\,^1/_2$ »
40. 9 $\times 5$ »
41. 5 $\times 16\,^1/_2$ »

PLATE X.

Strange horned figures in Val Fontanalba.

1. . . . . 26 $\times 15$
2. . . . . 33 $\times 19$

PLATE XI. - Weapons and Implements. Meraviglie Region.

Above the left bank of the Vallone.

1. 28½ × 7
2. 38½ × 9 ½
3. 35 × 12
4. 22½ × 8
5. 13½ × 3 ½
6. 28½ × 7
7. 40 × 8
8. 20 × 7
9. 28½ × 8 ½
10. 22 × 10½
11. 27 × 6
12. 42 × 12
13. 19 × 7
14. 22 × 5 ½
15. 30 × 8 ½
16. 15½ × 7
17. 34 × 21
18. 20 × 8
19. 26 × 9

Rock wall by the path.

20. 18½ × 7
21. 20½ × 7
22. 22 × 15½

Altar avenue.

23. 30 × 10½

South end of lake.

24. 52 × 12½
25. 16½ × 6 ½

South side of Altar Rock.

26. 17 × 8
27. 18 × 6
28. 18 × 8
29. 30 × 19 ½
30. 14 × 9

North side of Altar Rock.

31. 16 × 8
32. 38 × 16
33. 66 × 14
34. 30 × 7
35. 8 × 4
36. 50 × 6
37. 43 × 14
38. 16 × 7
39. 21 × 4
40. 28 × 9
41. 27 × 10
42. 13 × 8 ½
43. 22 × 5
44. 17 × 5
45. 99 × 27

Slopes of Monte Bego.

46. 49 × 8
47. 50 × 17
48. 27½ × 25
49. 22 × 24 ½
50. 15 × 5
51. 19 × 7
52. 14½ × 4 ½
53. 21 × 8
54. 34 × 21
55. 34 × 12
56. 24 × 6 ½
57. 36 × 30

Beyond the lake right bank.

58. 25 × 12
59. 31 × 9

South end of lake.

60. 27 × 7 ½
61. 38 × 12½

Between the lower and upper lakes.

62. 25 × 6 ½
63. 47 × 19½
64. 22 × 10
65. 18 × 13½
66. 23½ × 8
67. 22 × 10
68. 10½ × 8 ½
69. 18 × 6 ½

PLATE XII. - Weapons and Implements. Meraviglie Region.

Rock Waves.
1. 159 × 18
2. 106 × 26
3. 121 × 40
4. 43 × 12 ¹/₂
5. 64 × 28
6. 31 × 12
7. 29 ¹/₂ × 11
8. 33 × 10
9. 45 × 15
10. 24 × 6
11. 28 ¹/₂ × 17 ¹/₂
12. 22 × 9
13. 14 ¹/₂ × 12
14. 22 ¹/₂ × 17
15. 21 × 7

Near the Col.
16. 38 × 26
17. 20 × 7 ¹/₂
18. 36 × 6

Slopes above right bank of the Vallone.
19. 13 × 5 ¹/₂
20. 47 ¹/₂ × 8
21. 20 × 6 ¹/₂
22. 26 ¹/₂ × 6
23. 23 × 10
24. 31 × 21
25. 14 ¹/₂ × 5 ¹/₂
26. 17 × 12 ¹/₂

Slopes above right bank of the Vallone.
27. 42 ¹/₂ × 10
28. 14 × 5
29. 20 ¹/₂ × 4 ¹/₂
30. 48 × 25
31. 34 × 9
32. 38 × 10
33. 38 × 8
34. 15 × 7
35. 8 × 4
36. 25 × 42

Val Arpeto.
37. 44 ¹/₂ × 15
38. 24 × 14 ¹/₂

Near Lago del Carbone.
39. 44 × 20
40. 27 ¹/₂ × 7
41. 40 × 15 ¹/₂

Vallone della Rocca.
42. 25 ¹/₂ × 9 ¹/₂
43. 17 ¹/₂ × 10
44. 24 × 6
45. 15 ¹/₂ × 7
46. 19 × 7
47. 14 ¹/₂ × 6 ¹/₂
48. 32 × 11 ¹/₂
49. 22 ¹/₂ × 8
50. 20 × 12 ¹/₂

Vallone della Rocca.
51. 15 × 5 ¹/₂
52. 47 × 19
53. 15 ¹/₂ × 3
54. 21 × 5
55. 23 ¹/₂ × 5
56. 27 × 5 ¹/₂
57. 25 × 6
58. 24 ¹/₂ × 6
59. 25 × 4 ¹/₂

Arpeto Region.
60. 18 × 10
61. 26 ¹/₂ × 10 ¹/₂
62. 25 × 6
63. 32 × 10
64. 47 × 19
65. 21 × 13 ¹/₂
66. 18 ¹/₂ × 10

PLATE XIII. = Weapons and Implements. Val Fontanalba.

Via Sacra
1. 16 × 6 ½
2. 9 ½ × 6 ½
3. 7 × 3

Valley north of the upper Margheria.
4. 17 × 7 ½
5. 13 × 5 ½
6. 10 × 7 ½
7. 10 × 6

Santa Maria Rocks.
8. 21 × 13
9. 29 × 5
10. 20 × 5
11. 13 ½ × 4 ½
12. 26 × 7
13. 25 × 12
14. 44 × 18

Fork Rock.
15. 24 × 14
16. 14 × 4 ½
17. 13 ½ × 4 ½
18. 39 ½ × 10 ½

Castle Rock Ridge.
19. 32 × 10
20. 18 ½ × 5
21. 25 × 7 ½
22. 14 ½ × 3 ½

Below the upper lake.
23. 20 × 18

Above the upper lake.
24. 21 × 5

Upper smooth surface of the central mass.
25. 55 × 28
26. 35 × 32
27. 17 × 11

Middle smooth surface.
28. 15 × 17

Above the little gully.
29. 20 × 3
30. 13 × 15
31. 17 × 14
32. 25 × 5 ½

Central mass.
33. 25 × 6
34. 35 ½ × 18
35. 32 × 12
36. 43 × 11
37. 20 × 8
38. 40 × 16
39. 20 × 4

Above the little gully.
40. 34 × 8
41. 23 × 6
42. 16 × 6
43. 14 × 3 ½
44. 14 × 8
45. 19 × 5
46. 19 ½ × 6

Hillside beyond Lago Verde.
47. 14 × 5
48. 22 × 10 ½
49. 10 × 2
50. 24 × 5 ½
51. 24 × 6
52. 19 × 7 ½

Hillside beyond Lago Verde.
53. 49 × 10 ½
54. 44 × 9 ½
55. 35 × 8 ½
56. 21 × 9
57. 28 × 7
58. 17 ½ × 9 ½
59. 20 × 4
60. 15 ½ × 26
61. 36 ½ × 24
62. 24 × 12
63. 24 ½ × 24
64. 19 × 13
65. 11 ½ × 4 ½

Opening out of the big gully.
66. 12 × 12
67. 40 × 22

Amphitheatre beyond.
68. 30 × 7

Coscritti Rock.
69. 50 × 37

Skin Hill.
70. 35 × 8
71. 10 × 6 ½

S. Maria rocks.
72. 22 × 7

Little gully.
73. 17 × 5 ½

Armour rock.
74. 24 × 7

Big gully.
75. 54 × 30

Big Beast gully.
76. 19 × 11

Hillside beyond Lago Verde.
77. 14 × 13

PLATE XIV. - **Val Fontanalba.**

       1. 35×22.

       2. $35 \times 8^{1}/_{2}$ and 21×9.

PLATE XV. = **Vallone della Rocca.**

       Group of figures. 55×70.

PLATE XVI. - **Group of men with implements, called '*I Coscritti,*' in Val Fontanalba.** 50×37.

PLATE XVII. = **Group of figures with man called '*the Chief of the Tribes*' in Vallone delle Meraviglie.** 107×94.

PLATE XVIII. = Geometrical Figures etc. in Val Fontanalba.

Upper Margheria.	1. 17	$\times 16$	Central Mass.	27. 42	$\times 29$
Little Gully.	2. 40	$\times 16$	Near the big gully.	28. 45	$\times 37$
Via Sacra.	3. 25	$\times 23 \, ^1/_2$	Upper Margheria.	29. 24	$\times 13$
Great red S. Maria Rock.	4. 17	$\times 20$		30. 20	$\times 19$
	5. 32	$\times 15$	Little gully.	31. 24	$\times 17$
Little Gully.	6. 23	$\times 23$	Hillside beyond Lago Verde.	32. 28	$\times 38$
Upper Valley.	7. 20	$\times 7$	Foot of Great Red S. Maria Rock.	33. 36 $^1/_2$	$\times 23$
Central Mass.	8. 34 $^1/_2$	$\times 17$		34. 16	$\times 17$
Fork Rock.	9. 14	$\times 15 \, ^1/_2$	Middle smooth surface.	35. 17	$\times 15$
Great red S. Maria Rock.	10. 39	$\times 42$		36. 44	$\times 11$
	11. 12 $^1/_2$	$\times 21$	Central Mass.	37. 35	$\times 34$
Little gully.	12. 17 $^1/_2$	$\times 16 \, ^1/_2$	Via Sacra.	38. 30	$\times 16$
Big Beast gully.	13. 66	$\times 27$	Little gully.	39. 44 $^1/_2$	$\times 27$
Napoleon Rock.	14. 12	$\times 14$		40. 29	$\times 21 \, ^1/_2$
	15. 21	$\times 20$	Napoleon Region.	41. 16	$\times 16$
Fork Rock.	16. 27	$\times 36$		42. 31	$\times 22 \, ^1/_2$
Upper Valley.	17. 28	$\times 22$	Napoleon Rock.	43. 34	$\times 42 \, ^1/_2$
Central Mass.	18. 57	$\times 15$	Upper smooth surface.	44. 25	$\times 95$
	19. 48	$\times 14$	Below Great Red S. Maria Rock.	45. 51	$\times 41$
Great red S. Maria Rock.	20. 15	$\times 15$	Val Valauretta.	46. 20	$\times 120$
Central Mass.	21. 22	$\times 59$			
	22. 21	$\times 52$			
Hillside beyond Lago Verde.	23. 27	$\times 51$			
Napoleon Region.	24. 40	$\times 25$			
	25. 37	$\times 26$			
S. Maria Rocks.	26. 57	$\times 29$			

PLATE XIX.

Napoleon Rock. Val Fontanalba.
Enclosures with spots.

$$34 \times 42 \, ^1/_2$$

PLATE XX.
Skins etc. Val Fontanalba.

Skin Hill.
1. 24 × 12
2. 28 ½ × 21
3. 24 × 13
4. 28 ½ × 23
5. 59 × 27
6. 40 ½ × 23
7. 37 ½ × 32

Great Red S. Maria Rock.
8. 41 × 23 ½

Hillside beyond Lago Verde.
9. 13 × 9
10. 36 × 27
11. 30 ½ × 16 ½

Skin Hill.
12. 24 × 17

Marshy Valley.
13. 27 × 22

Skin Hill.
14. 65 × 42
15. 58 × 58
16. 60 × 65

S. Maria Rocks.
17. 65 × 40
18. 42 × 72

Great Red S. Maria Rock.
19. 320 × 142
20. 114 × 156

Upper Margheria.
21. 97 × 124
22. 93 × 82

PLATE XXI.
Val Fontanalba. 'Le Scale di Paradiso.'
119 — 82

PLATE XXII.
Geometrical Figures etc. Meraviglie Region.

Above the left bank of the Laghi Lunghi.
1. 21 × 53
2. 19 × 39
3. 17 × 28 ½
4. 19 ½ × 21
5. 13 × 10 ½
6. 16 × 25
7. 14 × 11
8. 25 × 105

Above the left bank of the Vallone.
9. 18 ½ × 28 ½
10. 12 × 28
11. 15 × 16
12. 17 × 40
13. 73 × 62
14. 104 × 53

Bird Rock.
15. 36 × 36
16. 14 × 22
17. 14 × 15 ½

Altar Rock.
18. 24 ½ × 14
19. 15 × 14
20. 28 × 34
21. 23 × 13
22. 26 ½ × 33
23. 27 ½ × 45
24. 16 × 12 ½
25. 20 × 19
26. 37 × 26

Slopes of M. Bego.
27. 13 ½ × 34
28. 47 × 37
29. 16 × 23

Near the Upper Lago.
30. 21 × 17
31. 11 ½ × 10
32. 7 × 15 ½

Rock Waves.
33. 26 × 39
34. 31 × 27
35. 26 × 14
36. 30 ½ × 20
37. 35 × 48
38. 32 × 36
39. 15 × 23
40. 19 ½ × 24

PLATE XXIII. = Geometrical figures etc. Meraviglie Region.

Rock Waves.	{	1. 68 $\times$ 49	
		2. 25 $\times$ 14 $^1/_2$	
		3. 29 $\times$ 69	
Altar Rock.		4. 20 $\times$ 25 $^1/_2$	
Rock Waves.		5. 36 $\times$ 33	
Défilé.	{	6. 35 $\times$ 52	
		7. 17 $^1/_2 \times$ 16	
Right bank of the Vallone.	{	8. 22 $\times$ 29	
		9. 14 $\times$ 28 $^1/_2$	
		10. 11 $^1/_2 \times$ 11 $^1/_2$	
Défilé.		11. 83 $\times$ 185	
Hillside above right bank of the Vallone.	{	12. 24 $\times$ 29	
		13. 47 $\times$ 67	
		14. 21 $\times$ 20	
		15. 8 $\times$ 22	
		16. 17 $\times$ 14 $^1/_2$	
		17. 12 $\times$ 11	
		18. 30 $\times$ 30 $^1/_2$	
		19. 28 $\times$ 20	
		20. 24 $\times$ 43	
		21. 26 $\times$ 36 $^1/_2$	
		22. 53 $\times$ 26	
		23. 24 $\times$ 52	

Vallone della Rocca. { 24. 8 $\times$ 11 $^1/_2$

Défilé. 25. 90 $\times$ 99

PLATE XXIV.

1. Rock in the Défilé
   35 $\times$ 52 and 37 $\times$ 26 $^1/_2$

2. Rivière's Rock. 47 $\times$ 67.

PLATE XXV. = Fontanalba Region.

Hillside near Lago di Paracuerta
1. $55\,^1/_2 \times 49\,^1/_2$
2. $51 \times 46\,^1/_2$
3. $22 \times 20\,^1/_2$
4. $15\,^1/_2 \times 9$
5. 35×37
6. $12\,^1/_2 \times 11\,^1/_2$
7. $11 \times 12\,^1/_2$
8. 7×7
9. $18\,^1/_2 \times 7\,^1/_2$
10. 9×15

Hillside farther west.
11. 26×7
12. $14 \times 11\,^1/_2$
13. 12×9
14. 21×11
15. 21×12
16. $13 \times 8\,^1/_2$

Slopes west of the Valletta di Santa Maria.
17. $17 \times 23\,^1/_2$
18. $20 \times 24\,^1/_2$
19. $39 \times 28\,^1/_2$
20. 13×39
21. $24\,^1/_2 \times 8\,^1/_2$
22. 38×9
23. 21×26
24. 16×21
25. 28×41

Via Sacra.
26. $6\,^1/_2 \times 8$
27. $6 \times 14\,^1/_2$
28. 12×9
29. $15 \times 5\,^1/_2$
30. 14×18
31. 15×10
32. 12×47
33. 26×39
34. 29×36
35. 8×12
36. 50×44
37. 34×21
38. 20×29
39. 86×100

By the upper Margheria
40. $26 \times 10\,^1/_2$
41. 18×22
42. 19×7

Between the upper Margheria and the two small ponds.
43. $27\,^1/_2 \times 17$
44. $20 \times 16\,^1/_2$
45. 28×15
46. 17×6
47. 41×41
48. 44×62
49. $12\,^1/_2 \times 9$
50. $13 \times 6\,^1/_2$
51. $6\,^1/_2 \times 6\,^1/_2$

PLATE XXX. = Fontanalba Region.

Marshy Valley and hillside.	1. $37\,^1/_2 \times 27$ 2. 23×17 3. 23×41 4. $31\,^1/_2 \times 16$ 5. $28 \times 27\,^1/_2$	Foot of the S. Maria Rocks.	26. 46×36
Skin Hill.	6. $14 \times 14\,^1/_2$ 7. $23\,^1/_2 \times 15$ 8. 21×37 9. 16×7 10. 9×6 11. 13×5 12. $25\,^1/_2 \times 19$ 13. $10 \times 6\,^1/_2$ 14. $34\,^1/_2 \times 18$ 15. 31×25 16. 45×25 17. 30×18 18. $41\,^1/_2 \times 28$ 19. 33×20 20. 52×38 21. 19×15 22. 48×32 23. $8\,^1/_2 \times 5$ 24. 36×15 25. $19 \times 14\,^1/_2$	First Ridge of the S. Maria Rocks.	27. 22×18 28. 33×19 29. 39×22 30. $43\,^1/_2 \times 15$ 31. 27×14 32. 28×15 33. 11×12 34. 121×133
		Second ridge.	35. 100×100 36. 21×11 37. 26×38 38. $21 \times 11\,^1/_2$

PLATE XXXII. = Fontanalba Region.

Third ridge of the S. Maria Rocks.	1. 28 ×12		Big Beast Gully.	27. 18 ×6
	2. 45 ×45			28. 64 ×33
	3. 36 ×13 ½			29. 15 ×24
The great red S. Maria Rock.	4. 84 ×23			30. 169 ×35
	5. 30 ½×20			31. 90 ×238
	6. 33 ×45		Upper great smooth surface.	32. 28 ×4
	7. 30 ½×25			33. 25 ×19
	8. 41 ×7			34. 23 ½×18 ½
	9. 35 ×10			35. 49 ×22
	10. 73 ×43			36. 26 ½×13
	11, 48 ×37			37. 19 ×16
	12. 67 ×142			38. 25 ×95
Castle Rock ridge.	13. 30 ×36		Middle great smooth surface.	39. 14 ×13
	14. 21 ½×9			40. 20 .×13
	15. 54 ×23			41. 48 ×42
	16. 80 ×32		Lower great smooth surface.	42. 23 ×9
	17. 21 ×16			43. 38 ×5 ½
By the stream.	18. 14 ×8 ½			44. 31 ×25
	19. 12 ½×6 ½		Southern part of the Central Mass.	45. 29 ×14
	20. 18 ×9			
	21. 38 ×39			
Elephant Rock.	22. 35 ×26			
	23. 21 ×23			
	24. 46 ×37			
Above the upper lake.	25. 23 ½×14			
	26. 16 ×16 ½			

PLATE XXXIV. - Fontanalba Region.

Middle and southern parts of the Central Mass.	1. 68 × 21
	2. 15 × 12 ½
	3. 54 × 24 ½
	4. 12 ½ × 5 ½
	5. 23 × 14
	6. 54 × 38
	7. 43 × 12 ½
	8. 12 × 10
	9. 29 × 23
	10. 26 × 17
	11. 51 × 40
	12. 82 × 62
	13. 23 × 18
	14. 18 × 8
	15. 13 ½ × 9
	16. 18 ½ × 8
Above Harrow Rock.	17. 68 × 20
Harrow Rock.	18. 59 ½ × 35
South = east corner.	19. 33 ½ × 30
Head of the Little Gully.	20. 51 × 27
	21. 43 × 40
	22. 10 × 11 ½
	23. 15 × 14 ½
	24. 27 × 19
	25. 31 ½ × 18
	26. 34 × 3
	27. 30 × 35

Head of the Little Gully.	28. 34 × 34
	29. 31 × 15
	30. 82 × 30
	31. 23 × 38 ½
	32. 28 × 53
Hillside beyond Lago Verde.	33. 51 × 35
	34. 35 ½ × 32
	35. 14 × 12
	36. 19 × 6
The 300 Rock.	37. 9 × 12
	38. 25 ½ × 17
	39. 19 × 10 ½

PLATE XXXV.

Hillside beyond Lago Verde.

1. Horned figure. 13 × 10.

PLATE XXXVII. - Fontanalba Region.

Hillside beyond Lago Verde.		Head of the Great Gully and Amphitheatre beyond.	Upper valley as far as the foot of Monte Bego.
1. 46 ½ × 37		29. 24 × 13	35. 21 ½ × 22 ½
2. 16 × 29		30. 24 × 20 ½	36. 17 ½ × 5 ½
3. 36 × 24		31. 78 × 15 ½	37. 16 ½ × 8
4. 33 ½ × 16 ½		32. 43 × 19	38. 30 × 17
5. 34 × 5		33. 23 ½ × 10	39. 25 × 16
6. 20 × 14		34. 30 ½ × 13	40. 9 ½ × 12
7. 46 × 22			41. 18 ½ × 9
8. 25 × 10			42. 16 × 12
9. 10 × 10			43. 31 × 26
10. 48 × 18			44. 42 × 12
11. 28 × 36			45. 18 ½ × 8
12. 56 × 17 ½			46. 34 × 13
13. 22 × 10			47. 12 × 4
14. 23 × 26			48. 39 × 25
15. 27 × 17			
16. 38 × 11			
17. 15 × 5 ½			
18. 19 × 55			
19. 13 ½ × 17			
20. 25 ½ × 30			
21. 11 × 7 ½			
22. 23 ½ × 11 ½			
23. 7 × 3 ½			
24. 11 × 5			
25. 60 × 16			
26. 23 × 8 ½			
27. 16 ½ × 3			
28. 33 × 14			

PLATE XXXVIII. = Meraviglie Region.

	Left bank / labels			Right labels	

Above the left bank of the Vallone.

1. $39\,^1/_2 \times 27$
2. $14 \times 18\,^1/_2$
3. 18×13
4. 17×15
5. 29×36
6. $17\,^1/_2 \times 9\,^1/_2$
7. 23×15
8. 9×6
9. $17 \times 8\,^1/_2$
10. $15\,^1/_2 \times 13$
11. $7\,^1/_2 \times 13$
12. $13 \times 9\,^1/_2$
13. 26×14
14. $32\,^1/_2 \times 18$
15. $37\,^1/_2 \times 16\,^1/_2$
16. 12×7
17. 22×35
18. 32×25
19. 42×33
20. 38×18

Near the path by the right bank.

21. 17×13
22. 15×12

Above the south end of the lower lake.

23. 20×12
24. 22×14
25. $28\,^1/_2 \times 25$
26. 27×17
27. 41×243

Bird Rock.

28. $15 \times 13\,^1/_2$
29. 18×18
30. $9 \times 23\,^1/_2$
31. $9\,^1/_2 \times 33\,^1/_2$
32. 9×33

South side of Altar Avenue.

33. 22×44
34. $29\,^1/_2 \times 8$
35. $46\,^1/_2 \times 13$

South side of Altar Rock.

36. $35 \times 18\,^1/_2$
37. 24×11
38. $22\,^1/_2 \times 12$
39. $25\,^1/_2 \times 22$
40. 12×45
41. 17×17
42. 19×13
43. $11\,^1/_2 \times 10$
44. $9\,^1/_2 \times 7$
45. 29×14
46. 15×44

Slopes of Monte Bego.

47. $22\,^1/_2 \times 29$
48. $24 \times 6\,^1/_2$
49. 21×11
50. 25×39
51. 22×14
52. $13\,^1/_2 \times 40$

PLATE XL.

1. Figure on the Rock Waves.
$30 \times 40\,^1/_2$

PLATE XLI. - Meraviglie Region.

Slopes of Monte Bego.	1. 27 $\times$ 32		Above the right bank of the Vallone	28. 13 $\times$ 13$^{1}/_{2}$
	2. 26 $\times$ 41			29. 11 $^{1}/_{2}$ $\times$ 11
	3. 14 $^{1}/_{2}$ $\times$ 17 $^{1}/_{2}$			30. 7 $\times$ 24 $^{1}/_{2}$
	4. 10 $^{1}/_{2}$ $\times$ 7 $^{1}/_{2}$			31. 13 $^{1}/_{2}$ $\times$ 6 $^{1}/_{2}$
Between the Lower and Upper Lakes.	5. 20 $\times$ 10			32. 14 $\times$ 6
	6. 27 $^{1}/_{2}$ $\times$ 16			33. 13 $^{1}/_{2}$ $\times$ 14 $^{1}/_{2}$
	7. 18 $\times$ 8			34. 24 $^{1}/_{2}$ $\times$ 36 $^{1}/_{2}$
	8. 7 $^{1}/_{2}$ $\times$ 4 $^{1}/_{2}$			35. 12 $^{1}/_{2}$ $\times$ 11 $^{1}/_{2}$
	9. 24 $\times$ 10			36. 38 $\times$ 12
	10. 21 $\times$ 14			37. 13 $\times$ 5
The Rock Waves.	11. 22 $\times$ 38			38. 28 $\times$ 34
	12. 29 $\times$ 18			39. 10 $\times$ 23
	13. 40 $\times$ 31			40. 13 $^{1}/_{2}$ $\times$ 36
	14. 40 $\times$ 24			41. 16 $^{1}/_{2}$ $\times$ 28 $^{1}/_{2}$
	15. 29 $^{1}/_{2}$ $\times$ 16 $^{1}/_{2}$			42. 32 $\times$ 13 $^{1}/_{2}$
	16. 30 $\times$ 40 $^{1}/_{2}$			43. 33 $^{1}/_{2}$ $\times$ 27
	17. 21 $\times$ 28			44. 7 $\times$ 7 $^{1}/_{2}$
	18. 28 $^{1}/_{2}$ $\times$ 14			45. 16 $^{1}/_{2}$ $\times$ 6 $^{1}/_{2}$
Rocks in the Défilé.	19. 19 $^{1}/_{2}$ $\times$ 30			46. 18 $\times$ 19 $^{1}/_{2}$
	20. 30 $\times$ 10			47. 11 $^{1}/_{2}$ $\times$ 29
	21. 12 $^{1}/_{2}$ $\times$ 15 $^{1}/_{2}$			48. 21 $\times$ 32
	22. 24 $\times$ 12			49. 16 $\times$ 11
	23. 21 $\times$ 17			50. 29 $\times$ 21 $^{1}/_{2}$
	24. 16 $\times$ 14			51. 16 $\times$ 22
	25. 24 $\times$ 19		Vallone della Rocca.	52. 19 $\times$ 11 $^{1}/_{2}$
Rivière's Rock.	26. 11 $\times$ 9 $^{1}/_{2}$			53. 23 $\times$ 17
	27. 17 $\times$ 2			54. 34 $^{1}/_{2}$ $\times$ 10 $^{1}/_{2}$
				55. 47 $\times$ 24

PLATE XLII. = Meraviglie Region.

Region	No.	Measurement
Vallone della Rocca.	1.	18 × 27 ½
	2.	18 × 27
	3.	21 ½ × 8
	4.	24 × 29 ½
	5.	19 ½ × 14
	6.	18 × 9
	7.	15 × 19
	8.	12 × 5
	9.	8 ½ × 8
	10.	13 × 7
	11.	15 ½ × 27
Arpeto Region.	12.	23 × 7
	13.	20 ½ × 17
	14.	16 × 13
	15.	35 ½ × 10
	16.	26 × 18 ½
	17.	21 × 15
	18.	28 ½ × 24 ½
	19.	18 ½ × 10 ½
Right Bank of Laghi Lunghi.	20.	11 ½ × 11
	21.	21 × 38
	22.	17 × 19
	23.	8 × 15
By Lago del Trem	24.	9 × 31
	25.	31 × 18
	26.	28 ½ × 20
Val Arpeto.	27.	13 × 11
	28.	49 × 33
	29.	40 × 16
	30.	107 × 94
Défilé.	31.	23 ½ × 16
	32.	19 × 54
Rock Waves.	33.	300 × 56
	34.	51 × 42
	35.	269 × 273
M. Bego slopes.	36.	54 × 37
Défilé.	37.	33 × 53
Altar Rock.	38.	49 × 45 ½

PLATE XLIII. = **Miscellaneous Figures.**

1. Rock by the stream from the Upper Lake.

    Val Fontanalba. 350 × 100

2. Hillside beyond Lago Verde. 132 × 79.
3.   »   Group of horned figures. 51 × 42.
4. Skin Hill Village. 97 × 36.
5. Near Napoleon Rock. 71 × 58.
6.   »   »   »   78 × 67.
7. Lower Lago delle Meraviglie. 22 × 23.
8. Head of the Little Gully.

    The smallest horned figure but one in the whole region. } 3 × 2
    Natural size.

PLATE XLIV.

1. Castle Rock ridge. 54 × 43.
2. Near the Upper Margheria. 67 × 42.
3. At the foot of the Great red S. Maria Rock. 86 × 82.
4. On Skin Hill. 232 × 96.
5. At the foot of the Santa Maria rocks. 217 × 117.

PLATE XLV.

1. The Monte Bego Village. 240 × 140.
2. On Skin Hill. 170 × 94.
3. The largest horned figure in Val Fontanalba. 316 × 99.

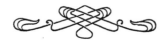

PLATE XLIV.

Groups of figures in Val Fontanalba.

PLATE XLV.

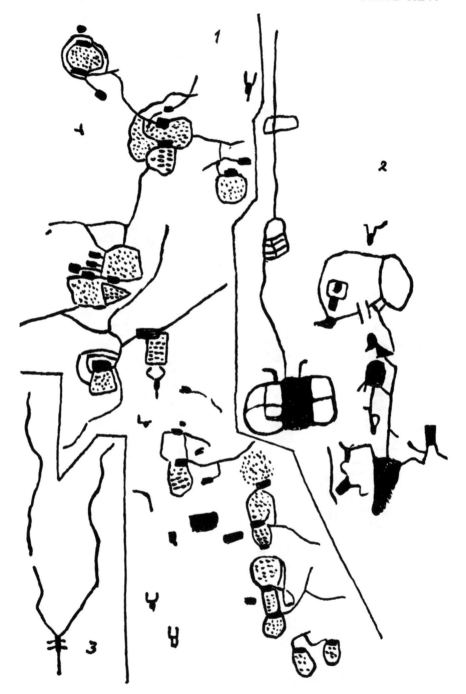

Figures in Val Fontanalba.
1. The 'Monte Bego village.' 2. Rock on 'Skin Hill.'
3. The largest horned figure in Val Fontanalba.

PLATE XLVI.

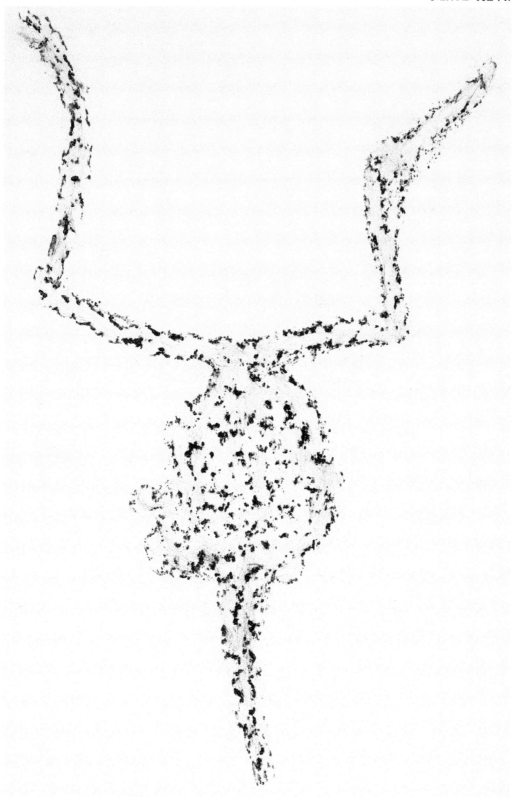

Heelball rubbing of figure from Val Fontanalba.

For EU product safety concerns, contact us at Calle de José Abascal, 56–1°,
28003 Madrid, Spain or eugpsr@cambridge.org.

www.ingramcontent.com/pod-product-compliance
Ingram Content Group UK Ltd.
Pitfield, Milton Keynes, MK11 3LW, UK
UKHW030901150625
459647UK00021B/2684